More Advance Praise for *Relic*

"Of all the books seeking to explain the decline of our political institutions, this one—from two of our best presidential scholars—might be the most radical. The problem, William G. Howell and Terry M. Moe argue, is that the Constitution fundamentally misdesigned Congress. Their cure for this mistake: a president with far greater control over the legislative process. For a daring argument about the future of American government, here's your book."

—RICHARD H. PILDES,
Sudler Family Professor of Constitutional Law,
New York University School of Law

"Marshaling an institutional imagination, *Relic* urgently contends that the Constitution should be revised to confer 'fast-track' powers on presidents to help American democracy successfully address our most pressing problems. Especially for those of us wishing to fortify Congress, this provocative call for a more formidable presidency offers a strongly argued challenge. Let the debate begin!"

—IRA KATZNELSON,
Ruggles Professor of Political Science
and History, Columbia University,
author of *Fear Itself: The New Deal
and the Origins of Our Time*

"Timely, accessible, and provocative, *Relic* is essential reading for scholars, policymakers, and ordinary citizens concerned about whether their government is up to emerging challenges like global terrorism, rising inequality, and climate change."

—ERIC PATASHNIK,
professor of public policy and politics,
University of Virginia, and author of *Reforms at Risk*

"Thinking constitutionally, Howell and Moe serve up a provocative and thought-provoking account of the major causes of our present discontents. Clearly written and engagingly presented, *Relic* promises to advance a badly needed conversation about how Congress and the President can constructively engage each other."

—SIDNEY M. MILKIS,
White Burkett Miller Professor,
University of Virginia

Relic

RELIC

★ ★ ★ ★ ★

HOW OUR CONSTITUTION
UNDERMINES EFFECTIVE
GOVERNMENT

———————

AND WHY
WE NEED A MORE
POWERFUL PRESIDENCY

WILLIAM G. HOWELL AND TERRY M. MOE

BASIC BOOKS

A Member of the Perseus Books Group
New York

Published by Basic Books,
A Member of the Perseus Books Group

Books published by Basic Books are available at special discounts for bulk purchases in the United States by corporations, institutions, and other organizations. For more information, please contact the Special Markets Department at the Perseus Books Group, 2300 Chestnut Street, Suite 200, Philadelphia, PA 19103, or call (800) 810-4145, ext. 5000, or e-mail special.markets@perseusbooks.com.

Designed by Janelle Fine

Library of Congress Cataloging-in-Publication Data
Names: Howell, William G., author. | Moe, Terry M., author.
Title: Relic : how our constitution undermines effective government, and why
    we need a more powerful presidency / William G. Howell, Terry M. Moe.
Description: New York : Basic Books, 2016. | Includes bibliographical
    references and index.
Identifiers: LCCN 2015048073 (print) | LCCN 2016001346 (ebook) | ISBN
    9780465042692 (hardback) | ISBN 9780465098583 (ebook)
Subjects: LCSH: Executive power—United States. | United States.
    Constitution. | United States—Politics and government. | BISAC: POLITICAL
    SCIENCE / Government / National.
Classification: LCC JF251 .H67 2016 (print) | LCC JF251 (ebook) | DDC
    320.973—dc23
LC record available at http://lccn.loc.gov/2015048073

10 9 8 7 6 5 4 3 2 1

For Marcy and Betsy
who anchor our lives and fill them with love

Introduction

Introduction

American government is dysfunctional, and anyone tuned in to politics sees evidence of it every day. As a decision-maker, Congress is inexcusably bad. It is immobilized, impotent, and utterly incapable of taking responsible, effective action on behalf of the nation.

So why is this happening? The most common view is that Congress's problems are due to the polarization of the Republican and Democratic Parties over the last few decades. By this rendering, if the nation could just move toward a more moderate brand of politics—say, by reforming primary elections or campaign finance—Congress could get back to the way it functioned in the good old days, when it (allegedly) did a fine job of making public policy. And then all would be well.[1]

But this just isn't so. Polarization has surely been detrimental to American government. Yet even if the political conditions of the good old days could somehow be re-created, it is wrong to think that Congress would then function admirably. The brute reality is that the good old days were not good. With relatively few exceptions, Congress has always been incapable of crafting effective policy responses to the nation's problems.[2]

Congress's most fundamental inadequacies are not due to polarization. Nor are they of recent vintage. They are baked into the institution. Congress is an irresponsible, ineffective policymaker largely because it is *wired* to be that way—and its wiring is due to its constitutional design. The Constitution ensures that members of Congress are electorally tied to their local jurisdictions, that they are highly responsive to special interests and narrow constituencies, and that these forces—which we will refer to, summarily, as *parochial* forces—profoundly shape their approach to policy. Congress as a whole reflects the parochialism of its members. It is not wired to solve national problems in the national interest. It is wired to allow hundreds of parochial legislators to promote their own political welfare through special-interest politics. And that is what they typically do.[3]

Much as Congress deserves to be everyone's favorite whipping boy, then, its pathologies are not really of its own making. They are rooted in the Constitution, and it is the Constitution that is the fundamental problem. The pathologies that the Constitution creates, moreover, are not limited to Congress. They extend to the entire system of governance. This happens, in no small part, because the Constitution puts Congress right at the center of the system by granting it the authority to make the laws, and its pathologies inevitably infect every other niche and component of government. Congress is not just one of three branches of government. The founders made Congress—and all the localism and special interests it channels—the *first* branch of government, expecting it to be the most important and consequential, with the second (the executive) and third (the judiciary) fully expected to trail behind.

These system-wide problems are considerably worsened by the very hallmark of the Constitution's approach to democratic governance: its much-celebrated separation of powers. The founders embraced separation of powers some 225 years ago, when the nation was a simple agrarian society of roughly four million people. Government was not expected to do much, and the founders—mainly worried about avoiding "tyranny of the majority" and other populist excesses—purposely designed a government that *couldn't* do much. Separation of powers was their structural means of accomplishing that. Its myriad checks and balances made governmental action very difficult and thus stacked the deck in favor of the status quo.

This approach to governance may have been fine for a simple agrarian society in the late 1700s. Or maybe not. Whatever the case, that time is long gone and it isn't coming back.[4] Americans today inhabit a profoundly different world. The United States of the twenty-first century is an exceedingly modern, postindustrial, highly interconnected, technologically advanced, fast-changing country that is awash in serious social problems—from terrorism to pollution to drugs to poverty, and on and on—that government is fully expected to address and try to resolve. Modern society also generates, quite inevitably, all sorts of basic social needs—for economic growth, a stable money supply, transportation systems, health care, retirement, education, and much more—that the government is called upon to deal with, and that can readily become serious problems if they are not handled well.

In today's times, these issues are very real, very pressing, and very consequential—and government must act, and act effectively, if it is to protect and promote the well-being of the nation. *How* it should act, of course, is a matter of partisan and ideological controversy. Liberals tend to favor top-down programs run by the government itself, and they tend to favor higher levels of spending and taxes. Conservatives are more likely to favor governmental approaches designed to give private-sector actors the incentives to mitigate the problems at hand, and they tend to favor lower levels of spending and taxes. Yet most conservatives and liberals can agree that—while their favored approaches differ markedly—government needs to take *some* sort of action in addressing the nation's major problems, and it needs to do so effectively. Whatever the policy approach, money should be spent wisely and efficiently, and problems should actually get solved.

American government lacks the capacity to do these things. Part of the reason, of course, is that separation of powers makes it difficult for government to act. Ours is a system of government in which power is parceled out, authority is divided, and the various branches of government, quite by design, are set against one another. But there is more to the government's incapacity than even this conveys. As we'll explain in the chapters to follow, the same constitutional wiring ensures that, when government does act, it tends to produce weak, cobbled-together, patchwork policies that lack coherence and are not effective. To make matters worse, even when those policies are shown—through actual experience—to be ineffective and greatly in need of fixing, they typically do not get fixed; they tend to live on despite their manifest inadequacies, creating an ever-growing conglomeration of programs that don't solve society's problems but continue to soak up society's resources.[5]

We can't blame the founders for any of this. They had no idea what modern society would look like, what its problems would be, or what kind of government might be appropriate for the modern era. They weren't clairvoyant. Indeed, they knew they weren't—and they assumed that, as society changed over time in whatever ways, future generations would change the Constitution to meet new and evolving needs.[6] But for the most part, future generations didn't do that. The Constitution—again, due to its original design—has proven difficult to amend, and fundamental changes to the organization of government have mostly been off the table.

The upshot is that the United States of today is burdened with a government designed for a bygone era. The times have radically changed, but the core of the Constitution—separation of powers, with a parochial Congress at its center—has not, leaving the nation with a government that is out of sync with the society it is supposed to be governing. It is a relic of the past.

Most of this book is devoted to explaining why this is so. The connection between the Constitution and ineffective government is not on the public's radar screen, and it needs to be. Huge majorities distrust the federal government these days. Many are sharply critical of the president. And Congress is regarded with thinly veiled contempt.[7] But the Constitution? It is above the fray—and above criticism, embraced with the kind of abiding reverence usually associated with religion. Public officials do bad things. The government does bad things. But the Constitution is good. And if the government and its officials fail the nation in various ways—which they do, regularly—then it is their fault, not the Constitution's.

Viewing the Constitution as beyond criticism is a big mistake. The Constitution is an antiquated document, imposed on modern America from the distant past, and it has enormous consequences for how the nation is governed, for how well it functions, and for countless important aspects of our everyday lives. There should be nothing off-limits about exploring the Constitution's impacts. These are matters of objective fact, and they need to be studied, assessed, and openly debated if Americans are to have a clear sense of why their government is disappointing them and what can be done about it. This book is our attempt to encourage new thinking along these lines.

We don't want to stop, however, with an analysis that points to the Constitution as a fundamental source of ineffective government. We also want to take the next step and consider what can be done about it. What can the nation do to bring its government into sync with modern times?

If we allow ourselves to pursue pie-in-the-sky alternatives, the possibilities are many. These would include the most obvious option: a parliamentary system—which is the form of government that prevails, with some variation, in every developed democracy but our own.[8] A reasonable case can be made that if the United States could design a new government from scratch, a parliamentary system of some kind would be superior to the separation-of-powers system our nation is burdened with now. It is not an accident that the countries of Europe and Scandinavia did not follow America's constitutional lead and that the new democracies of Eastern Europe, which formed in the 1990s, didn't either. As a practical matter, however, there is no chance that the United States is ever going to adopt a parliamentary system—or in any fundamental fashion, do away with separation of powers—as such a transformation would require a wholesale rewriting of the Constitution. So there is no point, here in this book, in considering these as live possibilities or assessing their merits.

At the other end of the spectrum are reforms that might be doable, such as those that we mentioned earlier, like addressing party primaries or campaign finance. But while these are much discussed nowadays, and while they surely direct attention to obvious problems afflicting American politics, they don't get to the most fundamental source of ineffective government, which is the Constitution.

In our view, the best path to major improvement is a middle course between these two extremes: a course that is pragmatic because it is within the realm of possibility, but also takes direct aim at the fundamentals that most need to be addressed. The problem is that the nation is burdened with an outdated Constitution. The solution is to update it. As we will show, this can be done in a way that is exceedingly simple, is low in risk, and leaves almost the entirety of the Constitution still in place—including separation of powers—but nonetheless promises to have great payoffs for effective government.

What we're suggesting, stated most generally, is a simple reform that makes Congress less central to the legislative process and presidents more central. The rationale for diluting Congress's importance is straightforward. Congress is wired to behave in ways that undermine effective government, and as a practical matter, nothing much can be done about that. Its members are rooted in their states and districts, they are wide open to special-interest influence, they are concerned about their own political welfare, and with rare exceptions they are collectively incapable of rising above their parochialism and fragmentation to craft truly effective policies for the nation. That being so, the path to effective government requires moving Congress from the front seat of legislative policymaking to the back seat, where its pathologies can do less damage.[9]

The nation is far better off with presidents in the front seat. Just as legislators are wired to behave in certain distinctive ways, so are presidents—but their wiring is very, very different, and it actually propels them to be champions of effective government. This is true regardless of whether the presidents are Republicans or Democrats, conservatives or liberals, insiders or outsiders. All presidents share basically the same wiring, and they can be counted upon to behave in the same basic ways.

Crucial features set presidents apart from members of Congress. The first is that presidents are truly national leaders with national constituencies who think in national terms about national problems—and they are far less likely than legislators to become captive to narrow or local special-interest pressures. They are politicians. They are not perfect. Their policy agendas won't please everyone. But compared to members of Congress, they are paragons of national leadership.

Second, presidents occupy the highest office in the land, having reached the pinnacle not only of their careers but of their entire lives—and as a result, invariably, they are strongly motivated by concerns about their legacies. Their legacies, in turn, are ultimately defined—by historians, most notably—not on the basis of day-to-day public opinion or short-term events but rather on the basis of demonstrated success in crafting durable, effective policy solutions to important national problems. Members of Congress are not driven by such lofty concerns. They are famously myopic, incremental, and parochial; they think about the next election; and they use policies for short-term and often local advantage.

Third, presidents are chief executives motivated and positioned to provide a coherent approach to the whole of government, whereas Congress can provide nothing of the sort. Its hundreds of members are mainly concerned about the various parts of government that matter to them as parochial politicians. Congress takes a piecemeal approach to the countless separate policies, programs, and agencies of government while presidents care about the entire corpus of government and about making it work.

For these reasons, presidents are wired to be the nation's problem-solvers in chief and to use the powers of their leadership to promote effective government. They have great difficulty, however, following through on these motivations. The Constitution sees to it—purposely, by design—that they are significantly limited in the formal powers they wield and heavily constrained by the checks and balances formally imposed by the other branches, particularly Congress. Presidents cannot require Congress to act, they don't control the legislative process, they can't determine the content of public policy—and the nation, as a result, is saddled with a constitutional system that makes it virtually impossible to take advantage of what presidents have to offer as the champions of effective government.

Something needs to be done about that. Fortunately, this challenge can be met without a radical transformation of the Constitution and a risky leap into the unknown. Under the reform we're proposing, the Constitution remains basically the same. So does Congress. So does separation of powers. The reform involves a simple, straightforward constitutional amendment that changes the way policy decisions get made: giving presidents broad and permanent agenda-setting power, and thereby moving Congress to the back seat of policymaking and presidents to the front.

A ROAD MAP TO THIS BOOK

Reform is called for when a system of government is mired in poor performance, as the American system surely is. In the usual course of events, reform proposals are a dime a dozen. Every pundit in the country seems to have ideas about what to do, and most of these ideas are either impractical or simply won't work to bring about significantly better government. If reforms are going to be successful, they need to be based on more than a recognition that the system is doing badly. They need to be based on an understanding of what is wrong. Only when it is known *why* a system is performing poorly, and thus what the fundamental sources of its problems are, can the nation—or anyone or any group—have a good sense of what changes will be most productive.

Our main purpose in writing this book is to promote such an understanding—and, in particular, to show that the Constitution lies at the heart of the nation's problem of ineffective government. In our view, the Constitution needs to be the focus of attention. It is the most fundamental source of the system's problems and the place to begin in really understanding them. The Constitution is more than two hundred years old, and for all its merits—which we recognize and admire—it imposes a structure of government on modern America that is woefully outdated and entirely ill-suited to the dynamics and demands of modern society. Its Congress is at the center of government—and pathological. Its separation of powers makes coherent, effective policy virtually impossible. Its presidents are champions of effective government, but heavily constrained and underpowered. The system as a whole doesn't work.

Our primary goal here, then, is to understand the nature of the problem—and only then, with that as a basis, to point the way out with a reform that flows from the same logic. This is a big job, and a serious one. It also requires that we cover a lot of ground. But we hope to do it in a way that readers find interesting and enlightening and that weaves a simple, seamless perspective on government that makes good sense and promotes understanding.

In Chapter 1, we discuss the ideas and values that went into the founders' original design of the Constitution, the kind of government they created for their simple agrarian nation, and the massive social and economic changes that took place during the late 1800s and early 1900s. These changes gave rise, quickly and dramatically, to a modern industrial nation wholly out of sync with an already outdated government, and in so doing spawned the most powerful movement for governmental reform the nation has ever seen: the Progressive movement, which swept American politics from about 1880 through 1920. The Progressives (who are not to be confused, we should emphasize, with the liberals of today)[10] were partially successful at creating a more modern form of government—led by a more powerful president—but the fundamentals of the original constitutional system remained intact. And as time went on, society continued to change at a dizzying pace, leading to an ever-widening gap between the needs of society and the capacities of government.

In Chapter 2, we focus on Congress during the modern era (mainly, from the mid-1900s through the 2000s), showing that it is often incapable of taking action on issues of crucial importance to the nation; that when it does act, it tends to produce cobbled-together policies that are ineffective at resolving the problems they supposedly address; and that when policies are known to have fixable flaws, the flaws don't actually get fixed, and the ineffective policies live on. Throughout, we illustrate these congressional traits with policy examples that range from health care to immigration to shipping to agriculture to education to welfare. And more.

In Chapter 3, we turn our attention to presidents. We explore what motivates them, why they are champions of effective government, what they have done throughout modern history to try to increase their power, and how they have sought to bring coherent policy change—typically in the face of daunting constraints and the usual minefield of congressional opponents. Here, too, we illustrate by discussing a range of substantive problem areas: climate change, social security, health care, and energy independence.

In Chapter 4, we present our proposal for reform. It involves a simple, well-tested decision model that moves presidents to the center of the policy process and stands to have big payoffs for effective government. We go on to consider the possible downsides, which are minimal, as well as whether it offers a feasible path to reform given the realities of American politics, which it does.

When all is said and done, what we most want to do in this book is to put the focus squarely on fundamentals. The Constitution was and remains a truly remarkable achievement in the history of human governance. But it was never designed to provide a government for modern America, and the nation is heavily burdened by the antiquated government it does provide. We are all prisoners of the past. Americans need to recognize as much—and do something about it.

1

The Constitution, Social Change, and the Progressives

Why is American government so ineffective? The answer can't be determined by staring at today's obvious dysfunctions—the partisan squabbling, the empty posturing, the almost complete inability to take action on serious social problems—and trying to figure out who or what is responsible for them. Nothing we can currently observe is really to blame in any fundamental sense. These things are symptoms, not causes. The causes have been there for ages, rooted in the Constitution.

Viewed objectively and shorn of the emotion people often bring to it, the Constitution is a few pages of rules and prescriptions, written more than two hundred years ago, that set out a design for American government and specify how its various components are supposed to operate. There was no guarantee at the time, nor has there ever been, that these rules and prescriptions would prove perpetually well suited to the governance of the nation. Indeed, by erecting an array of institutional impediments to lawmaking and putting Congress at the very center of its design, the founders built a government that would prove entirely ill-equipped to take on the challenges of a modern nation.

In order to make sense of today's failures of governance, therefore, we need to go back to the nation's beginnings and gain historical perspective. That is what we do in this chapter, but the ground that we cover here is more than just history. It is essential for understanding where the problems of today come from and how deeply rooted they are.

THE FOUNDERS' VALUES

The Constitution was written for a starkly different time, by men whose values and practical concerns were very much a product of that era. Like Americans of today, they valued democracy. And like Americans of today, they wanted a government that could effectively address the nation's pressing social problems. But these commonalities suggest a bond that is tighter and deeper than it really is. In fact, the authors of the Constitution did not think about democracy in anything like the way modern Americans do. And the practical problems they wanted the government to address were strikingly different as well. These differences in values and concerns are crucial. For the founders wrote the Constitution based on their values and their concerns, and we are living with the Constitution that they wrote.[1]

In the late 1700s the world was filled with nondemocratic forms of government, and the founders—living and acting in that context—were true champions of the cause of democracy and individual rights. Their values were revolutionary at the time. We might also say that, construed at a very abstract level, their values have proven to be timeless, in the sense that they continue to be embraced by Americans today, and indeed by people all over the globe.[2]

The Constitution powerfully advanced these timeless values. On a grand scale, for the citizens of an entire nation, the Constitution inaugurated the world's first democratic government.[3] And its Bill of Rights, added within the first few years, was a radical assertion that all citizens had certain inalienable rights that governments were bound to respect and uphold. By any standard, these were watershed developments in the history of human governance. Americans of that era could be supremely proud of what the founders had created. Americans today can be equally proud.

Yet we cannot put a halo over the Constitution—or the founders—and simply stop there. For once we get beyond the timeless abstractions of democracy and individual rights, it doesn't take much digging to discover that many of the founders' more specific ideas and values, if transported to the modern world, would be regarded by almost all Americans as totally unacceptable, and in some cases truly abhorrent. This is hardly surprising. The founders lived more than two hundred years ago, and we cannot expect them to have thought exactly as we do. Yet the differences are consequential for us today, and by paying attention to them we are better able to appreciate why having the founders speak for us—and design a government for us—is a formula that guarantees a bad institutional fit.

The kind of democracy the founders sought to create, and did create, was a very peculiar form of democracy indeed, one that probably would not even be called a democracy today. Part of the reason the founders were so undemocratic has to do with the particularly privileged social class from which they came. As a group, they were American aristocrats. Most were wealthy property owners and very privileged. George Washington, much admired then as now for his exploits on the battlefield and as the "father of our country," was one of the richest men in America. Many founders owned huge plantations or farms or were successful in business. Since the publication in 1913 of Charles A. Beard's controversial treatise, *An Economic Interpretation of the Constitution of the United States,* historians have wrangled over how profound a role the founders' own property interests and the protection of their privileged social positions played in their design of the Constitution. But by any reasonable account, most of the founders did not want—and indeed, feared—a democratic government in which ordinary citizens would actually have the power, through their votes, to engage in genuine self-government. As James Madison himself put it in Federalist, No. 10, such a democracy threatened to bring about "a rage for paper money, for an abolition of debts, for an equal division of property, or for any other improper or wicked project."[4] Some of these men, such as Thomas Jefferson and Benjamin Franklin, were more sanguine about popular control than others. And some, like Alexander Hamilton and John Adams, were even more worried about popular control than Madison and overt in wanting to put the American aristocracy securely in charge.

In approaching the design of a new constitution, then, the founders were faced with a difficult democratic puzzle—namely, as historian Richard Hofstadter put it, that "if the masses were turbulent and unregenerate, and yet if the government must be founded upon their suffrage and consent, what could a Constitution-maker do?"[5] The founders' solution to the puzzle, on the whole, was to favor a form of democracy that, by its formal architecture, would diffuse and weaken the political expression of populist sentiment and ensure that the public at large could not gain control of the new government.

As this jaundiced view of the public only begins to suggest, probably the most striking value gap separating the founders from modern Americans centers on the notion of political equality, and thus of who in a democracy should actually count. This is very much in evidence, as we will see, in the structure of government that the founders ultimately devised, in the central roles carved out for aristocrats like themselves, and in the very limited and indirect roles they provided for ordinary citizens. But it is also reflected in their approach to that most fundamental of democratic questions: who gets to vote?

The founders did not answer this question in their writing of the Constitution. They left it to the states to determine for themselves within their respective boundaries. But it is very clear that, although the founders expressed diverse ideas on this issue, they did not think about the right to vote—or political equality—as we do today. Most of the founders appeared quite comfortable with the notion that voting might well be restricted to white males who owned property (or paid a certain amount in taxes). This approach had been quite common across the states in the decades prior to the Constitution's adoption, and it continued to be common afterward—reflecting a widespread belief among leaders that voting should be restricted to stakeholders who had vested interests in the well-being of their states and communities, as well as the independence to resist corruption.[6] Madison was quite explicit that some deference to property made good sense, as there was a clear danger that those without property might use their political power for redistributionist ends.

Because America at that time was a rural nation of farmers, property ownership was high among white adult males, and the great majority of this particular group was qualified to vote in most states. But other Americans were not. Women were seen as having a proper place in the home and family but not in politics, and there was no general sympathy among the founders and other leaders for allowing women to vote. Among the states, only New Jersey did so—beginning in 1776 (although property restrictions were attached)—but the state legislature put an end to the women's vote in 1807.[7] There was little support for Native American suffrage. And while African American men who were free—and owned property—were allowed to vote in some states and localities, the overwhelming majority of blacks in America were slaves and, of course, could neither vote nor engage in politics in any meaningful capacity. Indeed, the Constitution specifically recognized slaves as but partial human beings—each counting as three-fifths of a person—for the purpose of determining how many representatives each state would receive in the new Congress.[8]

In juxtaposing these early times with our own, the exclusion of women from the right to vote is by today's standards an egregious violation of modern American values and an unjustifiable relegation of half the population to subordinate status. Important as that is, however, it is surely the slavery issue more than any other that crystallizes just how far the founders' values departed from our own. We could say, once again, that the founders were products of their times—and that the existence and perpetuation of slavery, given the historical context, shouldn't blemish their considerable democratic achievements. But to do so would give them more credit than they deserve. It is one thing for the founders to believe that only white male property owners should vote, and thus to deny women and others the right to participate on an equal basis. But it is quite another for them to allow—much less to actively participate in—the enslavement of other human beings. Anyone who thinks the founders were "like us" in their fundamental values would do well to ponder their tolerance of and involvement in slavery.

It might be comforting to imagine that the founders were essentially forced to accept a reality—concentrated in the southern states, backed by southern power—that they absolutely needed to accommodate if the thirteen states were to become one nation, and that they as moral individuals were horrified by slavery and wanted it eliminated. But this just isn't the case. Many founders were themselves slave owners—including, among many others, such prominent figures as George Washington, Thomas Jefferson, James Madison, John Hancock, John Jay, Patrick Henry, Richard Henry Lee, and Samuel Chase. No one forced them to own slaves. They did it voluntarily in their own economic interest. Many expressed qualms about slavery, even opposed it, in their public writings. But having qualms didn't stop them from owning slaves and doesn't somehow excuse them.

Slave-owning, we should note, was also exceedingly common among the first presidents of the United States. George Washington owned slaves throughout his presidency and continued to own them until the day he died. Thomas Jefferson also owned slaves throughout his presidency and was one of the largest slave owners in all of Virginia. Andrew Jackson, the iconic man of the people whose presidency is said to have signaled the rise of the common man, also owned slaves while president—and prior to that, he had actually been in the slave-trading business. Overall, of the first twelve presidents of the United States, ten were slave owners during their adult lives, most of them during their presidencies.

Only John Adams and his son, John Quincy Adams, rejected the institution of slavery in their deeds as well as their words.[9]

This is a sad and shocking history that historians are familiar with but that most Americans only dimly appreciate.[10] We recount it here not to denigrate the founders (or the early presidents) but simply to present them objectively and drive home the point that the age in which they lived was astoundingly different from ours, even when it comes to the most basic value of political equality. The founders often used much the same language as modern Americans in speaking about equality. Doubtless the most inspirational expression to be passed on to us from America's founding era is Jefferson's, from the Declaration of Independence: "We hold these truths to be self-evident, that all men are created equal." But as even the brief discussion provided here serves to illustrate, the founders did *not* believe that all men are created equal, and certainly not that women are the equals of men. Nor did they believe that ordinary people should control their own government, or even that most people should have any right to vote.

The Founders did believe in democracy, in a limited sense and at a very abstract level, which was a revolutionary thing for its time. But they feared the very people who populated their new nation. And as we will see, they purposely erected a government that kept ordinary Americans at a far and convoluted distance from real power. These were their values. In truly important respects, they are not the values of modern America.

A Practical Search for Effective Government

In writing the Constitution, the founders were acting on their values, but they were also doing something very practical in the context of their own lives: they were crafting a new government that they hoped would prove *effective* at meeting the basic needs of the new nation.

Since 1777, the thirteen states had been bound together by their first attempt at a constitution, the Articles of Confederation, but it had proven a miserable failure, putting the nation through "an unequivocal experience of the inefficacy of the subsisting federal government," in Hamilton's words.[11] The Articles had created a confederation of sovereign states, not an institutional structure that was capable of genuine governance. It had allowed for no executive leadership, no executive agencies, no judiciary, and no power to tax, and thus it had created a government too weak to address the basic and troubling problems that the states collectively faced at the time, including the debts of war, local rebellions, foreign threats, and a fragmented domestic economy. The founders wanted a new and very different form of government that would be capable of addressing these problems effectively, and they sought to write a new constitution that would give them one.

But they also feared governmental power. How, then, to proceed? They saw the challenge before them as a balancing act and an exercise in political engineering. Their job was to create, through structural design, a democratic national government with sufficient power to govern and take effective action—but not so much power that it could get out of control, dominate the states, and suppress individual liberties.

During their own era, the reality of governance throughout most of the Western world was one of monarchy and/or absolutism, and thus of excessive governmental power concentrated in the executive. One of the founders' great fears, then, was that in allowing for executive leadership through what would become the presidency, they might open the gates to despotism. They wanted an executive powerful enough to lead the new nation but not powerful enough to bring the threat of executive tyranny and the resurrection of the monarchy, or something like it. There would be no king for America. Their design of a new government would see to that.[12]

But executive despotism was not the founders' greatest fear. Their greatest fear was that democracy would lead to "tyranny of the majority," and thus that the legislature, if allowed to be the voice and vehicle of ordinary citizens, might well give rise to populist excesses that would threaten the rights of those not in the majority—including, notably, their property rights. The often turbulent and disruptive experiences of their own state governments, prior to the Constitution's adoption, helped to convince Madison and many others that these fears were well grounded. In his words, "the legislative department is everywhere extending the sphere of its activity, and drawing all power into its impetuous vortex."[13]

The problem with the legislature—which, as the lawmaking body, would stand at the center of their government—ran deeper than its potential control by majorities. The deeper problem was that it stood to give powerful expression to the many "factions" in society that would inevitably seek to use government to their own ends. And "the latent causes of faction," Madison observed, "are sown in the nature of man. . . . A zeal for different opinions concerning religion, concerning government, and many other points . . . [has] divided mankind into parties, inflamed them with mutual animosity, and rendered them much more disposed to vex and oppress each other than to co-operate for their common good."[14] In designing a new government, then, the most fundamental challenge was to control what Madison called the "mischiefs of faction," which were associated with threats to property and the ominous prospect of tyranny of the majority. The legislature was not to be trusted and was especially dangerous. But the executive was not to be trusted either. In fact, *no one* was really to be trusted because all people from all walks of life were inclined to act in their own special interests and, indeed, might well try to dominate others if given half a chance.

So what kind of government might possibly work? The founders' solution was a government that no one could actually control—no person, no faction, no simple majority. The government would operate *as a system*, whose outputs—laws for the nation—would be generated through the interdependent actions of a host of differently situated, potentially antagonistic players. The key principle in designing such a system to public advantage lay in Madison's dictum: "Ambition must be made to counteract ambition."[15]

The way to do this, he and the other founders determined, was through a separation of powers. The core functions of government—the legislative power to make the law, the executive power to implement the law, and the judicial power to interpret the law—would be formally placed in separate branches of government. Each would exercise certain powers that were uniquely its own. But their powers would also overlap, allowing them to check and balance one another. This would actually be a governmental system, as political scientist Richard Neustadt described it many years later, of "separated institutions sharing power."[16]

Historically, the founders were the first to put such a governmental scheme into national practice. But in figuring out how to proceed, they weren't flying blind. Instances and discussions of "mixed" governmental arrangements, of which they were well aware, went back at least to Aristotle and the Roman Republic.

The thirteen colonies had various forms of mixed governments themselves, offering vivid examples that the founders studied in detail. And influential thinkers of their era, including John Locke, William Blackstone, and Montesquieu, made strong arguments for limited government that the founders much admired. Montesquieu—nearly a contemporary, dying in 1755—was their guiding spirit. He was the one who most fully developed the theory of three separate branches of government and checks and balances. He also argued for dividing the legislature into two houses: one elected by commoners, one composed of noblemen and propertied elites, with the consent of both needed to pass any given law, thus allowing each house to check the other *within* the legislative branch.[17]

THE CONSTITUTION

Under the intellectual leadership of Madison, the new American Constitution would bear the indelible stamp of Montesquieu's ideas. Given a political world in which no one could be trusted, not even the majority of American voters, separation of powers seemed to square the circle. In the eyes of the founders, it allowed them to create a government with sufficient formal power to be effective at addressing the problems of their day. At the same time, it allowed them to create a government whose power was so ingeniously parceled out that ambition would counteract ambition, no faction could tyrannize over others, and personal liberty and property would be secure.

The founders recognized Congress as the first branch of government and granted it the single most important power in the new American republic: the power to make the laws. But the founders created a divided institution. The House of Representatives would reflect the interests of ordinary people, and its members—apportioned by population—would be elected by voters in local districts. The Senate, by contrast, would give equal weight to each of the states—large and small, regardless of population— and its members, expected by the founders to be prominent elites like themselves, would be chosen by state legislatures. Both chambers would need to consent for a bill to become law, allowing each chamber to check the other in protecting its distinctive constituencies. Most important, the Senate could block any populist excesses that might arise from the more democratically based House, providing an immediate line of defense against "tyranny of the majority."[18]

Congress was the centerpiece of the founders' new government. But the nation also had a great need for executive leadership—for the energy, dispatch, and capacity for action that the Articles had failed to provide and that Congress as a collective institution could not provide either. To meet that need, the founders created the presidency.[19] As they did, there was much debate over just how powerful the new president should be, with Hamilton the lead advocate for a stronger presidency and a more centralized political system and Madison arguing for a weaker presidency and a more decentralized system based on states' rights. But on the whole, as they worried about the dangers of executive tyranny, the founders strove for balance and constraint.

The Constitution vested the "executive power" in the hands of the president, making him the government's manager in chief. Consistent with that role, the president was authorized to appoint high-ranking administrative officials. Yet the Constitution also stipulated that he do so with the "advice and consent" of the Senate, which, in practice, empowered the Senate to reject his preferred candidates, insist on others, and impose long delays before positions could actually be filled. Similarly, the Constitution recognized the president as commander in chief of the armed forces. Yet Congress was empowered to declare war, as well as to determine how much money, if any, would be devoted to such an effort, further constraining the president's leadership in this most crucial realm of national policy. Just as Congress could check the president, however, so the president could check Congress. Most significantly, the president was empowered to veto legislation (subject to a two-thirds override by both houses).[20]

The founders saw great value in presidential leadership. They never intended, however, for the president to be a tribune of the people. On the contrary, they shielded the office from popular pressures that might arise from ordinary Americans. Presidents were to be elected not through a direct vote, but rather by an Electoral College of elite "electors," whom the states would choose in whatever manner their legislatures deemed appropriate.[21] As the founders saw it, the selection of the president was too important to be placed in the hands of everyday citizens.

The third branch of government, the judicial, would be led by the Supreme Court and manned by federal judges who would be appointed for life—because the founders wanted them to be above politics. While Congress and the president were jointly empowered to make the laws, the courts were empowered to review and interpret those laws, as well as to nullify any they believed were contrary to the Constitution. Even when Congress and the president agreed that a given law should be adopted, then, the lawmaking process would not really be over because the courts would later have opportunities to specify the law's meaning and even to eviscerate or overturn it, thereby checking the lawmaking powers of the other branches—and possibly giving rise to outcomes that neither Congress nor the president intended.

Separation of powers, therefore, stood at the core of the founders' new government. But it was not the whole of it. The system contained two additional components that introduced even more complexity and constraint. The first was federalism. The states entered into the Constitution with long histories of self-governance, so they were naturally intent on keeping much of their autonomy. Under the new design, they would be equally represented in the Senate. The Senate would therefore be an egregiously undemocratic institution—giving Delaware's 50,000 free residents, for example, exactly the same clout as Virginia's 516,000—but it would also provide the states a formal power base from which to protect themselves against encroachments by the central government.[22] Under the Bill of Rights, moreover, the Tenth Amendment stipulated that all powers not granted to the national government would be reserved to the states—guaranteeing them a key role in the nation's public policy and creating yet another power base for resisting federal encroachment. Thanks to federalism, then, the national government would be limited and encumbered in ways that go well beyond separation of powers.

The second component, along with federalism, was the entirety of the Bill of Rights, the first ten amendments to the Constitution, which were proposed almost immediately (by Madison in 1789) in response to Anti-Federalist concerns about the centralized power of the federal government and ratified in 1791. The Bill of Rights enumerates freedoms and rights that the federal government cannot abrogate, such as the freedoms of speech, religion, press, and assembly; the right to due process; the right to a jury trial; and the right to keep and bear arms. These provisions not only restrict what the federal government can do but also magnify the power of the Supreme Court—for it is the Court that determines what these restrictions mean in the practice of governance, and there is so much ambiguity inherent in their wording that the Court inevitably has enormous discretion in imposing its own views on the rest of government and thus in shaping the direction and possibilities of public policy.

EFFECTIVE GOVERNMENT?

As a novel experiment in limited government, the Constitution was a beautifully conceived antidote to the absolutism and predation that the founders so feared. Government would function as a complex system of interdependent parts in which all relevant factions, interests, constituencies, and classes would participate—yet none would be able to dominate. There would be no tyranny of the majority, no American monarchy. Liberty and property would be protected. Government would be controlled by its own internal checks and balances.

But would this design also give the nation an *effective* government? Not just for 1789, but for 1889, 1989, and on into the future? To answer these questions, we need to recognize that, if a government is to be effective, it must have the capacity to take coherent action in response to pressing social problems that need to be addressed and resolved—which requires, at a bare minimum, that it be capable of passing appropriate laws. *To act, governments must pass laws.*

Given this simple framing, we are faced immediately with a contradiction that pits the Constitution against effective government:

stripped to its essentials, the most fundamental thing that a separation of powers system does is to make the passage of laws extremely difficult. If a legislative proposal is to become law, it must pass the House, pass the Senate, not be turned back by the president, and not be overturned by the courts. These are all veto points. If an opposing group, however small and unrepresentative, can prevail at just one veto point at any step along the way, the proposed law will be blocked and governmental action will be prevented. Action will only be taken when all the relevant factions can agree on what to do. In this way, the Constitution purposely stacks the deck in favor of the status quo and in favor of only those governmental actions that can gain broad consent.[23]

This deck-stacking was strongly reinforced as the internal dynamics of the system worked themselves out in subsequent decades of actual governance. Each chamber of Congress developed a committee system to do its work, which added layers of complication to the legislative process; the Senate developed rules to allow for filibusters, which let a minority of its members stop a bill in its tracks; and other opportunities to impede the production of laws, whether by anonymous holds or in conference committees, only proliferated.[24] So too, therefore, did the opportunities for blocking, and for insisting that bills be weakened, altered, distorted, or gutted in order to get a diverse range of actors and interests on board. Such outcomes are especially important to understand and appreciate. For separation of powers doesn't just undermine effective governmental action by preventing any action at all. It also undermines it by ensuring that, when government *does* act, its laws will often be cobbled-together concoctions that are crafted as they are for political reasons, to attract disparate politicians with disparate interests into the "support" coalition, but are weak and incoherent as actual means of addressing social problems. (In later chapters, we will explore this phenomenon in some detail.)

Due to the design of the Constitution, the incentives for the various actors to use these opportunities to block bills or cobble together laws on political rather than programmatic grounds were built into Congress from the very beginning. Representatives were electorally accountable to their local districts and thus to the constituents, interests, and power holders therein. Senators were accountable to the constituencies, interests, and power holders in their states. The result was an unleashing of far-flung parochial pressures in which members of Congress used whatever means were at their disposal—committees, procedures, floor votes, logrolling (vote-trading)—to bring home the bacon to their districts and states and to block, weaken, or reshape any legislative proposals that didn't fit their parochial interests. The entire legislative system was deeply—and permanently—rooted in parochialism.[25]

Why, then, would such a design have been adopted in the first place? Wasn't it obvious from the very outset that a separation-of-powers system, especially one with such parochial foundations, would fail to provide an effective government capable of addressing the nation's problems and promoting the national interest?

The answer is: no, it wasn't obvious at all—and indeed, in the context of colonial America, it may not even have been true, at least not to a debilitating extent. One reason is that the Articles of Confederation set a very low bar. Almost anything would have been more effective than the Articles. The new government was clearly more powerful than the old one, with explicit legislative, executive, and judicial branches of government. It was more centralized, with national-level authority for containing the centrifugalism of the thirteen states. It was a major improvement over what came before.

Another reason the Constitution stood to be more effective is that the broad consent necessary for governmental action was easier to arrange in those early years, and parochialism less disabling. By comparison to modern times, the country was very small and relatively homogeneous, particularly among the small subset of people who could actually vote. Critically, moreover, the number of key political players was quite manageable. The first US Congress consisted of just twenty-six voting members of the Senate and sixty-four members of the House—small numbers compared to today's political system (100 in the Senate, 435 in the House), making compromise and cooperation easier to orchestrate.

But the most important reason that separation of powers may have offered the founders a tolerably effective form of government was that they lived in a very simple agrarian society—and government was not expected to do much. "Effective" meant something very different in those early times than it means today. The founders sought to create a government that could carry out the most basic of functions. Notably, they wanted a government that could defend the nation against external attack, promote internal security (by preventing, for example, another Shays' Rebellion against government-levied taxes), ensure the states' compliance with foreign treaties, regulate commerce and trade between the states in basic ways (for example, by ensuring that they didn't erect tariffs against one another), collect customs to raise revenue, and provide citizens and businesses with certain basic services, like mail delivery and financial help with the construction of turnpikes and waterways.

That was essentially it. Society was simple. Government wasn't expected to do much—and it didn't do much. In that kind of world, separation of powers stood to provide a government effective enough to meet the expectations and demands of the time. But what kind of world was that, exactly, and how does it compare to the world we know today? In truth, the two are as different as a horse cart and a Tesla.

In the early United States, the entire country had a population of some four million people (including about seven hundred thousand slaves), 95 percent of whom made a living from farming and other rural pursuits. This tiny population was spread out thinly across the thirteen states, with a density of just 4.5 people per square mile, including slaves. There were cities, but they were remarkably small by today's standards. New York City was the largest, with just thirty-three thousand residents, followed by Philadelphia, with twenty-nine thousand, and Boston, with eighteen thousand. And while these urban areas were important centers of business and finance, they were entirely unrepresentative of the nation as a whole, which was overwhelmingly agricultural and rural.[26]

The modern United States looks nothing like that. The nation stretches geographically from the Atlantic to the Pacific (and beyond), with fifty states and a population of more than three hundred million. In terms of people alone, the nation is now seventy-seven times bigger than it was in 1790. It is also a highly urban, industrialized, interconnected—and complex—society, knitted together by freeways, airlines, television, and (not least) the Internet. Farming is controlled by huge agribusinesses, and only a minuscule number of Americans—roughly 1 percent—make their living off the land. The population density, despite the extraordinary increase in land mass since 1790, has soared from 4.5 to 87.4 people per square mile. The average lifespan has more than doubled, from 34.5 years to 76.4 years for men and from

36.5 years to 81.2 years for women. Cities have become huge and sprawling, and they dominate the economic, social, and cultural landscape of the nation. New York City claims more than eight million residents and is 242 times larger than it was in 1790. Los Angeles—which didn't exist in 1790, its land area then controlled by Spain—now has four million residents: roughly equal to the total population of the United States when the Constitution was adopted. Altogether, there are now ten cities with populations above one million and thirty-four with populations above five hundred thousand.[27]

Today, the nation's economy is many orders of magnitude bigger, more complex, and more diverse than it was in 1790. In real (inflation-adjusted) terms, the GDP has grown from a mere $4.3 billion to some $18 trillion. In other words, the GDP of today is roughly *four thousand times greater* than the GDP of 1790, a truly mind-boggling measure of just how different our world—and all its social complexities, social interdependencies, and social problems—is from theirs. Imports have grown from $553 million to $2.6 trillion, and exports from $460 million to $2.1 trillion (meaning that both are about 4,600 times greater than in 1790). Globalization and the revolution in information technology have brought about levels of economic exchange between nations, including almost instantaneous capital flows and communications, that were previously unthinkable. Indeed, they were unthinkable just a few decades ago.[28]

The United States today also occupies a dramatically different place in the international order. At the nation's founding, leaders were surely concerned about relations with other countries, particularly Britain and France, and about the dangers of war. But the United States was also separated from these nations by a vast ocean, isolationist tendencies ran strong in its politics, and American citizens were preoccupied with getting their domestic affairs in order. The founders, therefore, created a government that was barely equipped to engage in foreign affairs. The State Department retained all of seven full-time employees (who included, in addition to Secretary Thomas Jefferson, a chief clerk, three other clerks, a translator, and a messenger), and the military, for its part, supported just one thousand soldiers. Things could not be more different today, obviously, as the State Department bulges with almost seventy thousand people on its payroll and the military employs some 1.3 million. More generally, whether measured by the size of its economy, the strength of its military, the diplomatic influence it wields, or the cultural attractions it produces, the United States is nearly unrivaled on the international scene, and this has been true for roughly a hundred years. Throughout this time, as the "leader of the free world," the United States has been expected to monitor, if not resolve, nearly every issue of consequence occurring around the globe—be it tidal waves drowning Indonesian coastlines, border disputes between Ecuador and Colombia, regional trade patterns in the Pacific Rim, terrorist threats in the Middle East, or most anything else that arises.[29]

In these and countless other respects, modern American society is profoundly different from the colonial society of the founders. And it inevitably generates serious social problems (as well as attractive social opportunities) that modern citizens fully expect government to address. Of course, conservatives and liberals often disagree about exactly what the government should do and how it should do it. Conservatives tend to argue for responses involving greater reliance on markets and incentives (within, inevitably, a framework designed and imposed by government).

Liberals tend to argue for greater reliance on government rules and public bureaucracy. But there is widespread agreement across the ideological spectrum that government needs to take some sort of action—whatever the specific tools, means, or mechanisms— to manage the economy, mitigate poverty, support senior citizens, clean up the environment, subsidize health care, enforce civil rights, aid the unemployed and disabled, direct air traffic, operate prisons, control drugs, oversee securities and financial markets, regulate agricultural markets, take care of veterans, educate children, train workers, manage and protect national parks (and other public lands), regulate international trade, provide disaster relief, fund and generate research, collect a broad range of statistics, and on and on and on. And then there are all the functions associated with foreign affairs, national security, and the conduct of diplomacy and war, which add enormously to the government's responsibilities and to its need to take effective action on behalf of the nation.

If government is to address the myriad problems that arise in the modern world, it must be able to act, and act effectively. But it literally wasn't designed for that. It was designed for a very different, premodern world. It is folly to think that what may have worked quite well in that world will also work in ours. Why would it? The founders had no idea what a modern society would look like, no idea what demands and problems it would generate, no idea what governmental effectiveness would require in such a context. They could not provide us with a government suitable for modern times even if they intended to.

And they didn't intend to. They explicitly saw themselves as engaging in an experiment in governance for their times, and they expected and encouraged future Americans to revise and adjust the

Constitution over time as conditions warranted.[30] The problem isn't that the founders somehow failed future Americans. The problem is that future Americans didn't take ownership of the Constitution and update it for their own times. The nation is left, as a result, with a constitution that was designed for another world and is wholly out of sync with modern society.

A Changing Society and a Changing Government

There is nothing unusual about a constitution falling out of sync with its society, especially over a long timespan. In fact, as influential scholarship by Samuel Huntington, Francis Fukuyama, and others has shown, this sort of thing is exceedingly common for governmental institutions generally, across nations and time.[31]

Consider what has been happening in modern China. Its communist government shifted toward a market-driven economy during the 1980s with tremendous success, leading to spectacular growth rates, massive increases in personal income and urbanization, and the rise of an urban middle class. But the Chinese government is now out of sync with its own fast-modernizing society, which generates demands for information, openness, innovation, the rule of law, and freedom of speech and action that are precisely what the communist government is institutionally wired *not* to provide, and indeed is wired to resist, repress, and punish. If the Chinese government isn't radically changed to come into congruence with its society, the nation's progress will ultimately be limited and stifled. Burdened by inappropriate institutions, its economy will eventually plateau, and ordinary Chinese citizens will suffer for it.[32]

The institutional dilemma we're describing here is quite general. It emerges because all government institutions, everywhere, are designed for specific social contexts at specific points in time—but any congruence between institutions and their contexts is unlikely to last. The reason is simple but profound. On the one hand, institutions tend to be stable: they regularize behavior and relationships, coordinate expectations, are protected by vested interests—and for these and other reasons are very difficult to change. On the other hand, the societies these institutions are designed to govern *do* change. And over a period of time, they may change quite radically, generating new interests, new constituencies, and myriad new problems that the prevailing institutions weren't designed to deal with. The result is that the prevailing governmental institutions, while perhaps very well designed for their own eras, can get increasingly out of sync with their societies as time passes, leading to degraded levels of performance. Something has to give. Societies need to renew and reconfigure their institutions to be congruent with the new conditions—or suffer the consequences of stagnation and decay.

This is precisely the bind the United States is in today. It is not a bind, however, that is new. It has actually been plaguing the nation for a very long time. In important respects the Constitution was flawed from the beginning because it failed to deal adequately with the slavery issue and, in adopting a separation-of-powers arrangement filled with opportunities to block policies, failed to provide any governance mechanisms for resolving it over the decades—leading to the Civil War and the near destruction of the United States as a nation. But slavery was a uniquely horrible problem from the outset, rooted in powerful, geographically concentrated, well-represented vested interests, and it is not clear that slavery would have had a political solution under a different constitutional rubric.

The best way to appreciate the Constitution's long-standing and growing incongruence with American society is not to focus on the Civil War as a critical test of governmental effectiveness, but rather to focus on the more mundane, continuous, relentless processes of modernization that have shaped the nation throughout its history, and would have done so with much the same consequences (for incongruence) had slavery never existed.

From the very start, change was fast in coming.[33] The geographic size of the nation doubled right away, in 1803, with Jefferson's Louisiana Purchase, which pushed the frontier as far west as what is now Colorado, Wyoming, and Montana. Subsequent additions—the Republic of Texas in 1845, the Oregon Territory in 1846, and the Mexican Cession in 1848—quickly created a country that spread from the Atlantic to the Pacific and dwarfed the original thirteen states. When Jefferson made the Louisiana Purchase in 1803, he believed that it would take one hundred generations for Americans to populate this new expanse of western territory. He was spectacularly wrong. Within less than three generations—not one hundred—the West would expand all the way to the Pacific, and countless thousands of Americans would participate in the California gold rush, set up farms and businesses, and sink roots in this wild and untamed territory that teemed with opportunity. When the Constitution was adopted, 95 percent of Americans lived east of the Appalachians. By 1860, a full half of all Americans lived west of the Appalachians. And the nation had thirty-three states, not thirteen.[34]

Meantime, the American economy was developing apace. The new western lands contained vast natural resources and created a huge common market ideal for economic trade and growth across regions. Turnpikes, canals, and early railroads were built, first in the Northeast and later elsewhere, to facilitate transportation and exchange. Innovations—the cotton gin, machines for spinning and weaving cotton thread, the sewing machine, machines for canning food, the mass production of firearms, the steamship, and many others—ramped up production and trade, shifted more production from households to factories, and moved the nation along an upward economic trajectory. Cyrus McCormick's mechanical reaper, patented in 1834, along with newly developed mechanical seeders and threshers, promoted the mechanization and commercialization of American agriculture, along with major increases in productivity and the shipping of products to faraway markets.

These economic developments were accompanied by changes in the population and its composition. The US population doubled between 1790 and 1820 with almost no help from immigration, which had largely been shut off due to foreign wars. After that it took off as immigrants streamed in over the next several decades: from 130,000 in the 1820s to 600,000 in the 1830s to 1.7 million in the 1840s to 2.6 million in the 1850s—most of them from Germany and Ireland, all of them seeking a better life in a new land. By 1860 the nation's population had grown to 31 million. And with economic development and the growth of commerce and industry, its cities had grown as well, both in size and in economic and cultural prominence. New York City (including Brooklyn) was by this time a city of one million residents—and thus was already some thirty-three times larger than it had been in 1790. Philadelphia's population had grown to 566,000, Boston's to 178,000. Eight cities now had populations exceeding 100,000—including Cincinnati, St. Louis, and Chicago in the "West."[35]

As the nation changed socioeconomically, its core institutions, for all intents and purposes, remained fixed. The basic designs of

Congress, the presidency, and the courts looked much as the founders had originally made them. American politics, though, underwent dramatic changes. The Constitution does not mention political parties, and the founders did not envision that they would emerge and become key organizers of American government. But that is what happened, of course, and it happened almost immediately. As soon as the new government began operation with Washington as president, the nation's political elites congealed into Federalist and Republican factions, and these factions functioned as political parties—a rational and inevitable response to their strategic need to control votes and policy. The Federalists, led by Washington, Hamilton, and Adams, supported a stronger and more active central government—as reflected, for example, in their support for a national bank—and they were associated with commercial and business interests and with the northern states. The Republicans (later called the Democrat-Republicans), led by Jefferson and Madison, favored states' rights and a much weaker central government and were anchored in rural, agricultural interests and the South.[36]

The dominance of elite-based parties, however, was not to last. With the vast increase in the nation's geographic reach, the rapid rise in population, the influx of immigrants, and the intoxicating influence of democratic ideals among the commoners, state governments moved toward universal male suffrage. And in this context, elites saw great value in building political parties capable of reaching out and mobilizing this large, fast-growing electorate. With Andrew Jackson's election as president in 1828, the Democrats—an evolution of the agricultural, southern-based Republican party of Jefferson—became the nation's first mass party, followed in short order by the Whigs (based in the North and in commerce, as the Federalists had been) and later the Republicans (replacing the Whigs and running on an anti-slavery platform).[37]

Jackson ushered in the so-called age of the common man. This label is a gross misnomer, really, as the common man still had little influence over government. But even so, the shift away from the earlier aristocratic control was sharp and consequential. A new political era had begun, and with it came a new era for government. With parties now mass-based organizations rather than simple coalitions of elites, armies of political activists were needed to round up voters and maintain their support both during and between elections, and these activists could be attracted and paid off by giving them government jobs. When parties won elections, then, they used their control of government to dole out public jobs to their loyalists—"to the victor go the spoils"—and thus filled the bureaucracy with employees whose only qualification was that they had performed electoral duties for their party. The federal bureaucracy, as a result, became populated by party hacks, rendering the bureaucracy itself, almost from the very beginning of its existence, entirely incapable of carrying out any but the most basic functions, like delivering the mail. Members of Congress, meantime, were products of their parties, beholden to them and up to their necks in a patronage system that—despite its destructive effects on government—benefited them as politicians.[38]

The same problem afflicted American governments at the state and local levels, where party machines—the local power bases of national politicians—became entrenched in cities and statehouses across the country. Through their electoral control of governments, parties simply used government money and jobs to build their own organizations, win elections, and feather their own nests through countless forms of graft and thievery. This was democracy in America, and it wasn't pretty. While state and local governments sometimes played positive roles in economic development—helping to fund roads and canals, for instance (the Erie Canal being a prime example)—they tended to be grossly lacking in competence and expertise. Parties controlled and looted government to their own advantage. And virtually all the major power holders were in on the game, and benefiting from it, with no incentives to change. This was a bad system, but a system very much in equilibrium.

The saving grace was that, aside from fighting the Civil War— and battling, at times, Native Americans and Mexicans—the federal government was not called upon to do much. It could be incompetent and parochially driven in its own restricted realm, but the private sector—which was almost totally unregulated and unrestricted—was where the real action was taking place, and the private economy and the nation's civil society of independent farmers and small businesses was flourishing nicely. In most respects, the federal government was not crucial to citizens' lives or to the nation's prosperity. The United States was rich in land, resources, ambition, and opportunity, and it could grow and succeed without an active or effective national government.[39]

MODERNIZATION AND A GOVERNMENT OUT OF SYNC

But in the last half of the nineteenth century, a booming American private sector changed all that forever. With the Civil War over and the nation finally at peace, innovation and industrialization raced ahead at a furious pace, transforming and boosting the national economy in countless realms of production: railroads, iron and steel, petroleum, chemicals, coal mining, sugar, machinery, meatpacking, and much more. Big business reigned as newly formed corporations amassed unprecedented capital and power, and complex organizations became much more common, rationalized, and efficient. By 1900, the nation's real GDP was five times what it had been in 1860.[40]

Agriculture grew far less labor-intensive through technological change and mechanization and also grew more productive and commercialized. In the process, the republic of self-reliant farmers championed by nearly every president from Jefferson to Lincoln was increasingly diluted and marginalized. Whereas four times as many Americans lived in rural as in urban areas in 1860, that ratio plummeted over the next decades. By 1920, for the first time in US history, more than half the nation lived in towns or cities with populations of 2,500 or more.[41]

Cities mushroomed in size and complexity as workers flocked from farms to urban factories and immigrants arrived in record numbers to man mostly low-wage urban jobs—adding not only to the nation's workforce but also to its ethnic and religious diversity. Some fifteen million immigrants landed on the nation's shore from 1860 to 1900, at which point a full third of the nation was either foreign-born or children of the foreign-born. In many cities, these new arrivals made up a majority of the population. Another 14.5 million immigrants arrived between 1900 and 1920, reinforcing these transformational trends.[42]

Small businesses proliferated to meet the burgeoning demands of the new urban society, and they formed the backbone of a rising, increasingly vocal and demanding middle class—the hallmark of a modern society and a new and growing stratum of citizens who tended to be better educated, more attuned to politics, less tolerant of corruption and party machines, and more insistent on clean, effective, democratic government. Paralleling this rise of the American middle class, labor unions emerged to represent the industrial working class—the American Federation of Labor, most notably, was formed in 1886, led by Samuel Gompers—as employees complained of low wages, abysmal and unhealthy working conditions, and all manner of exploitation by their new bosses. Strikes and other labor conflicts became commonplace.

As all these changes (and more) were occurring, massive infrastructure was being built. Railroads and telegraph lines knit the sprawling nation together through an ever-thickening web of communication and transportation that began to integrate even the most rural and remote pockets into the national economy, greatly facilitating trade, shipping, and travel and making the various sections of the country interdependent in ways they never had been in the past. Between 1860 and the mid-1870s, the number of miles of railroad tracks doubled, reaching from coast to coast. By 1890, it had doubled again. At about that time, the telegraph network throughout the country was well-enough developed that a merchant in New York City could telegraph an order for goods to San Francisco and (thanks to the railroads) expect to receive it within a week. Americans, wherever they were, were now truly one nation, part of a common whole.[43]

The modernizing developments of the first half of the 1800s were surely significant. But the wrenching changes of the second half of the century were of a markedly different order, generating a tectonic shift that transformed a simple agrarian society into a modern industrial society, one far more complex, diverse, interconnected, urban, industrial, middle class, and cosmopolitan. And along with this cataclysmic upheaval in the nation's socioeconomic order came a complex array of vexing social problems that were virtually nonexistent in the past but were now very real—and impossible for Americans and their leaders to ignore.

The free-market economy that had so successfully propelled industrial growth was now plagued by monopolies, price-fixing, and "trusts." Wealth and power had suddenly become exceedingly concentrated, with the new barons of industry and finance—John D. Rockefeller, Andrew Carnegie, Jay Gould, Cornelius Vanderbilt, J. P. Morgan, and a few others—wielding enormous influence over the nation's economy and its politicians. The money supply was subject to political manipulation and threatened nationwide booms and busts. Farmers suffered from the rapacious actions of the railroads. Corruption was rampant. Sweatshops proliferated. Children worked long hours under horrible conditions, as did many immigrants, coal miners, and factory workers. Workers were beaten, fired, and thrown in jail for trying to form unions. Medicines were often fraudulent and dangerous. Meat processing was often filthy and a threat to public health. Public lands were being snatched up, developed, and plundered. Cities desperately needed roads, sewage systems, water systems, electricity, public transportation, and other basics of urban life. And on and on.[44]

From today's standpoint, these sorts of social problems are regarded as so egregious and so basic that there is virtually universal agreement that they need to be dealt with, and dealt with effectively, *by government*. As we've said, today's conservatives and today's liberals would endorse different policy approaches, depending on the issue. But both would recognize that the national economy cannot be left entirely to the free market, that the money supply cannot go unmanaged, that child labor is unacceptable, that public lands need to be protected, that drugs need to be regulated, and that in these and many other very basic ways, government needs to act—perhaps through its own agencies, perhaps through selective reliance on the private sector or some other innovative means—to address the serious, often dangerous problems that modern society inevitably generates.

In the late 1800s, however, government was not acting. Society was in the throes of a radical transformation, beset by massive problems that called out for governmental action—but it was burdened by a premodern institutional apparatus that was simply not capable of dealing with the situation. Part of the reason is that, with the rise of party machines and the spoils system, American government was so parochial and corrupt that it had little motivation to address these vexing new problems, and it was so incompetent that it couldn't have even if it wanted to.

Beneath the parties, the corruption, and the incompetence, though, there was a more fundamental reason that American government was incapable of meeting the challenge of modernity: the Constitution was now seriously out of sync with the underlying society. The founders did not foresee that, a hundred years in the future, the nation would be profoundly transformed by the rapid advance of industrialization—and that this transformation would unleash a torrent of social problems that would require a response if the United States was to have a healthy economy, if its democracy was to be genuine, and if Americans were to lead prosperous, safe, and happy lives. The government they created in the late 1700s—based on separation of powers and deeply rooted in parochialism—was designed for *that* era, and for a premodern social environment the founders well understood. But with the passage of more than a hundred years, that environment had been transformed into something entirely different, and the government they had created, a government designed to prevent and obstruct coherent action, was simply not suited to this new, modern setting.

What the nation needed at the dawn of the twentieth century was a government well designed for the social environment of its times. Instead, the nation was saddled with an anachronism, a throwback to a bygone era that couldn't hope to deal effectively with the problems and challenges of modern society.

THE PROGRESSIVE RESPONSE

This disconnect between government and society, along with the ineptitude and failure that it exposed, gave rise to the Progressive movement, which emerged in the late 1800s and proved to be the most powerful and consequential movement for governmental reform that this country has ever known.

Animated by the demands of the middle class, small businesses, and civic associations, inspired by the disruptive ideas of influential intellectuals, and mobilized and directed by forceful political leaders—Theodore Roosevelt, Robert La Follette, and Woodrow Wilson most notable among them—Progressivism was above all else an insistence on "good government," a goal that translated into two central aspirations. The Progressives sought a more genuinely democratic government, one responsive to ordinary people rather than powerful special interests. And they sought a more effective government, one capable of addressing the ever-deepening problems of modern America.[45]

Progressives revered the Constitution and its democratic values, as everyone did. But from the movement's earliest stirrings, its key thinkers also saw the Constitution's architecture as unworkably outdated, imposing institutional arrangements that were disabling in a modern setting—and serving, in effect, as a formal straitjacket that prevented the government from solving big and looming societal problems. As the Progressive historian Herbert Croly put it, "The economic and social changes of the past generation have brought out a serious and a glaring contradiction between the demands of a constructive democratic ideal and the machinery of methods and institutions, which have been considered sufficient for its realization."[46]

Perhaps the most influential Progressive thinker was Woodrow Wilson, who would become president in 1913 but achieved prominence much earlier as an academic, beginning with his now-classic work, *Congressional Government*, published in 1885. In this book, Wilson took aim at Congress, arguing that it was a parochial institution, fragmented into autonomous, self-serving committees, and inherently incapable of providing coherent policy solutions to pressing national issues. But his main attack was on separation of powers more generally, and thus on the core of the Constitution itself, which he saw as the ultimate source of the political system's inability to act in a coherent, effective way. "Power and strict accountability for its use are the essential constituents of good government," he wrote. "It is, therefore, manifestly a radical defect in our federal system that it parcels out power and confuses responsibility as it does. The main purpose of the Convention of 1787 seems to have been to accomplish this grievous mistake."[47]

Wilson was hardly a wild-eyed revolutionary. He was very much a man of the system—elected twice to the presidency and before that elected governor of New Jersey—but he was also a trenchant critic of that system. Throughout his careers as an academic and a politician, Wilson remained attentive to the urgent challenges that the dramatic modernization of American society posed for the traditional political system, and he wrote at length about how Progressives saw the brave new world in which they suddenly lived and why the old approach to governance would no longer work. In this excerpt from his 1913 book, *The New Freedom*, Wilson identifies the crux of the problem:

> Nothing is done in this country as it was done twenty years ago. We are in the presence of a new organization of society. Our life has broken away from the past. . . . The old political formulas do not fit the present problems; they read now like documents taken out of a forgotten age. . . .
>
> We have come upon a very different age from any that preceded us. . . . We used to think in the old-fashioned days when life was very simple that all that government had to do was to put on a policeman's uniform, and say, "Now don't anybody hurt anybody else." We used to say that the ideal of government was for every man to be left alone and not interfered with, except when he interfered with somebody else; and that the best government was the government that did as little governing as possible. That was the idea that obtained in Jefferson's time. But we are coming now to realize that life is so complicated that we are not dealing with the old conditions, and that the law has to step in and create new conditions under which we may live, the conditions which will make it tolerable for us to live.[48]

The problem, as Wilson and other Progressives saw it, was that the law could not step in to create those new conditions as long as the nation was saddled with an outmoded, ill-suited form of government. So what could they do?

Constitutional amendments were much discussed, and a few were even adopted—which, given the enormous obstacles faced by any amendment effort, is itself a testament to the historically unusual power of this movement. The Seventeenth and Nineteenth Amendments did away with anachronistic restrictions on democracy by, respectively, providing for the direct election of senators (in 1913) and giving women the right to vote (in 1920). The Sixteenth Amendment (in 1913) allowed for a national income tax and thus expanded the government's revenue base—a prerequisite for active government.

The core features of the Constitution, separation of powers in particular, were not going to be amendable, and that being so, the Progressives sought to modernize American government as best they could by working within the system. They targeted much of their reformist energy at state and local party machines—whose power, corruption, and iron grip on public office holders, including members of Congress, had long made good government impossible—by promoting reforms like the direct primary, the secret ballot, and civil service. The result, over subsequent decades, was the virtual destruction of American parties as powerful organizations. Without the ability to control their own nominations, the parties could not control who ultimately won office and made policy. And without the ability to mete out spoils, they could not attract the troops necessary for getting out the vote and controlling elections. So the parties withered—and the age of the entrepreneurial politician was born.[49]

The Progressives also sought to build the administrative capacity of government. Until the Progressive era, the American bureaucracy was tiny, underdeveloped, and filled with patronage employees (most of them postal workers). But the Progressives recognized that an expert, competent, well-functioning bureaucracy is a hall-mark of modern government and the organizational means by which it ultimately acts to convert legislative words into something real, concrete, and consequential. The core of their reform strategy, which dovetailed perfectly with their strategy to weaken the parties, was to replace the spoils system with merit-based civil service. They won their first big victory in 1883 with the Pendleton Act, and the movement for civil service was ultimately successful—but the vested-interest opposition was so great that it took roughly fifty years for merit-based civil service to fully take hold. More generally, the Progressives pushed for a government that put greater responsibility in the hands of administrative experts and bureaucratic agencies, and they argued strongly—consistent with their anti-party, anti-politics, anti-spoils theme—for a "separation of politics and administration" that would allow administrators to apply their objective, expert judgment in making good government a reality. Some of the most noteworthy Progressive achievements in this push for administrative capacity were the new federal agencies they created, including the Interstate Commerce Commission to regulate the railroads, the Federal Reserve to regulate the money supply, the Federal Trade Commission to regulate anticompetitive business practices, the United States Forest Service to regulate the nation's forests, the National Park Service to regulate the (then new) national parks, and what later became the Food and Drug Administration to regulate food and drugs, among others.[50]

Most important for our purposes, the many Progressives who embraced Wilson's seminal critique of American government also recognized that Congress, as a collective bicameral body rooted in parochialism, was inherently incapable of providing the nation with coherent leadership—and that effective government in the modern era called for a much more central and powerful role for the president.[51] Liberated from the control of party machines and patronage, the president would be motivated by national problems and the larger public interest, could take action decisively and with coherence, and could be held directly accountable by the people. No longer should presidents be in the shadow of a parochial, fragmented Congress. They should *lead* Congress— and lead the nation.

The views of Henry Jones Ford on such matters are emblematic of Progressive thinking on this point. According to Ford, any meaningful evaluation of the nation's political institutions required a careful assessment of their ability to solve problems. And on Ford's accounting, Congress at the dawn of the twentieth century had become the "shuttlecock of politics," a cesspool of political factions wherein posturing substituted for deliberation and local and personal interests displaced well-meaning efforts to confront genuinely national problems. But whereas Congress invited nothing less than "shame" upon its members, Ford thought, the presidency was something altogether different. Mitigating the impediments to problem-solving within Congress, Ford was convinced, required not rehabilitating the House or Senate but elevating the presidency. According to Ford, the president and the president alone could break through the bramble of congressional politics. As he put it, "The evidence which our history affords seems conclusive of the fact that the only power which can end party duplicity and define issues in such a way that public opinion can pass upon them decisively, is that which emanates from presidential authority." Without the presidency, our national politics would consist of little more than partisan squabbles and sectional strife. And without a strong presidency, national interests could not be expected to prevail.[52]

The very embodiment of these Progressive ideals was Theodore Roosevelt, who assumed office in 1901 upon the assassination of William McKinley and radically reshaped popular expectations of what presidents could and should be doing. Roosevelt was active, aggressive, and very public in identifying serious national problems that needed to be addressed, in demanding policy solutions to those problems, and in acting to pressure, cajole, and threaten Congress into passing the policies on his agenda.[53] As the nation's problem-solver in chief, he was a trustbuster, going after the railroads and the titans of industry; he was a consumer advocate, taking action to regulate drugs and food; he was an environmentalist, creating a system of national parks; and much more. And as aggressive as he was in domestic policy, he was at least as aggressive in foreign policy. He was, in fact, the first US president to be truly recognized as a world leader. Among other things, he built the Panama Canal (and, in so doing, fomented a revolution that "liberated" Panama from Colombia), announced the Roosevelt Corollary to the Monroe Doctrine (justifying US intervention in Latin American affairs), and secretly mediated the end of the Russo-Japanese War (for which he was awarded the Nobel Peace Prize).

During his time in office, Roosevelt acted upon what he later called his "stewardship" theory of the presidency, which holds that presidents have the duty to take whatever steps they think necessary to promote the nation's best interests unless they are specifically prohibited by explicit language in the Constitution or statute. In this view, legal ambiguity allows presidents—indeed, invites them—to fill the void and take charge of national policy. In an autobiographical reflection on his own actions as president, Roosevelt observed, "Under this interpretation of executive power I did and caused to be done many things not previously done by the president and the heads of departments. I did not usurp power, but I did greatly broaden the use of executive power."[54]

Woodrow Wilson had very much the same view of the presidency. As he put it, "The President is at liberty, both in law and conscience, to be as big a man as he can. His capacity will set the limit." Indeed, once the nation moved beyond the laissez-faire 1920s, all future presidents took much the same approach. With Progressivism, presidential leadership and the expectations surrounding it were forever changed.[55]

FROM PROGRESSIVISM TO TODAY

It is common to date the advent of modern American government to Franklin Delano Roosevelt and the New Deal. For it was then, during the crisis of the Great Depression, that the nation first developed its own version of the modern welfare state, government regulation vastly expanded, and the administrative component of government grew enormously in size and scope. But the New Deal was built on a foundation constructed by the Progressives. They were the ones who ushered American government into the modern era—not in response to economic crisis but in response to the relentless forces of social and economic modernization that were fast transforming the nation.[56]

Faced with this tectonic shift in society, what the Progressives achieved over a period of several decades—roughly from 1880 to 1920—was a tectonic shift in *government*, yielding a new institutional arrangement that was clearly a much better fit with the newly industrialized America. The government of old was designed to do virtually nothing. It was filled with party hacks, devoid of administrative capacity, dominated by a parochially based Congress, and constrained by a strictly interpreted, antiquated Constitution—all of which generated a government that simply could not address national problems in an effective way. The Progressives sought to change all that. And they were remarkably successful. Their reforms weakened and eventually destroyed the party machines and the spoils system, and they gave rise to a presidentially led bureaucratic state that was far better equipped to deal with the problems of modern society.[57]

This victory of Progressivism took place a hundred years ago. There has been no comparable shift in government since then. Important changes have taken place, to be sure. Most significantly, presidents have grown increasingly powerful, they have gained more control over the nation's policy agenda as "chief legislators," and they—not Congress—are universally turned to as the nation's problem-solver in chief. That the government has the authority to take action in addressing the nation's problems, and indeed should take such action, is widely embraced throughout American society.[58] And there is now a well-developed administrative state, ostensibly under the president's direction as chief executive, that affords government the means of turning legislative words into concrete outcomes.

The nation owes a great thanks to the Progressives. They gave us a modern government. Yet we need to recognize that their reforms were only partially successful. The most significant and lasting achievements, after all, did not alter core features of the Constitution itself. Rather, they affected the terms under which government officials were hired and fired, the strength of parties, and the prevalence of patronage and corruption. In the wake of their efforts, the fundamentals of the Constitution remain firmly in place. Congress still makes the laws, is still mired in localism and special-interest pressures, and is still lodged at the center of American government. And the political system as a whole is still filled with institutional roadblocks that prevent it from taking effective action to address the nation's problems. The Progressives, moreover, were dead wrong about some things. They were naive, for example, in believing that administration could somehow be separated from politics and that policy can reliably be entrusted to experts in bureaucratic agencies—because the bureaucracy, as we will later discuss, is heavily influenced by Congress and its parochialism, and hence is heavily politicized. The Progressives also failed to realize that, in destroying the parties as organizations, they were creating a vacuum that interest groups would rush to fill—and that modern American government would be just as susceptible to special-interest pressure as the premodern government they sought to escape.

That the Progressives were only partially successful should hardly come as a surprise. They were not all-knowing, and they were operating in a political world that made (and still makes) institutional reform extremely difficult. Partial success, under the circumstances, is a big deal. But even that partial success has been subject to erosion. For although the Progressives' extraordinary accomplishments helped to bring government more fully into sync with American society in the early 1900s, society has continued to change—and the changes have been massive, complex, and explosive in their proliferation.

The Progressives sought to forge a government that could deal with the most basic problems of the early industrial age. But we now live in an age in which government must deal with a mind-boggling array of profoundly troubling and consequential issues: of terrorism, intense international competition, rapid and disruptive technological innovation, rising inequality, persistent poverty, climate change, and much more. What the nation needs is a government that can be nimble, responsive, and effective at addressing these problems of a much-evolved modern world. But it clearly does not have one.

Once again, Americans are burdened with a government that was designed for a bygone era, by designers who had no idea what society would look like or what its problems would be a hundred years in the future. The challenge for today—as it was for the Progressives—is to see the disconnect between government and society for what it is, and to try to do something about it.

2

Congress and the Pathologies
of American Government

Let's take a closer look at the government that the founders bequeathed us some 225 years ago and see how the institution at its very center—Congress—functions in modern times. Today, it's easy to ridicule Congress for its gross ineptitude, its routine inability to manage everyday affairs, and the cleavages that yield such dissent within and across the two major parties. But if we are to take the full measure of Congress, we might as well evaluate it at its very best. And during the modern era, the legislative engines have never run as smoothly or with such gusto as they did during Lyndon Johnson's early years as president. Then, the political parties weren't polarized, huge Democratic majorities controlled both chambers of Congress, and laws were passed like they were going out of style.[1]

During this brief period, Congress enacted a handful of landmark laws, most notably the Civil Rights Act of 1964 and the Voting Rights Act of 1965. But aside from these truly exceptional bills—which Congress only managed to pass, we need to recognize, a full hundred years after African Americans were supposedly granted the rights of citizenship—what did the content of Congress's policies actually look like during this special time? Congress was at the top of its game. It had everything going for it. Did it gear up to produce coherent policy solutions to the nation's many problems?[2]

For answers, let's consider one of the signature pieces of legislation that emerged from this heady era of sky-high congressional productivity: the Model Cities program.[3] This program was an integral part of President Johnson's War on Poverty, through which he sought to come up with effective policy solutions that would attack the nation's poverty problem on multiple fronts. To do that, he created task forces of people with deep knowledge and experience. One of these task forces dealt with the dire state of the nation's cities, which were reeling from violence, riots, white flight, and crumbling infrastructure. The idea this task force came up with was truly novel. Arguing that past federal programs had spread their money too thinly across too many cities to do any good, it proposed a completely different approach: an experimental program in which the federal government would *concentrate* a sizable amount of urban redevelopment money on a small number of especially needy cities—five or ten, perhaps fewer—to see if targeted infusions of big money could turn these "model cities" around.

The task force soon came face to face with a brute political reality: its proposal stood no chance of making it through Congress unless the number of cities was expanded so that more senators and representatives would see money flowing into their own states and districts. Indeed, Senator Abraham Ribicoff (D-CT), the only elected official on the task force, argued for expanding the number of cities to a full fifty—so that each member of the Senate might expect to get a model city. But then, of course, there was the House to win over as well. So, bowing to political reality, the task force issued a final report proposing sixty-six model cities, hoping that this distortion of its original idea would pave the way for passage.

In early 1966, President Johnson sent his Model Cities legislation to Congress, setting off an intense struggle. The result was a blizzard of amendments that compromised the task force's core idea still further—but succeeded in producing a new law. The amendments guaranteed the selection of small cities (even towns), not just large urban areas. They limited any state's portion of money to 15 percent of the national total, ensuring that smaller states would share in the flow of funds. And most important, they more than doubled the number of cities (and towns) from the already vastly inflated number proposed by the task force.

So, yes, Congress gave the nation a new law whose supposed purpose was to address the problem of urban decay. Yet, as the political scientist R. Douglas Arnold notes, "the final program hardly resembled the one conceived by the presidential task force. An experimental program of five to ten cities was transformed into a program benefiting 120 to 150. . . . The whole idea of concentrating large amounts of money in a few cities had been replaced by a congressional desire to spread the same funds among many cities."[4] One of the model cities receiving money, for example, was MacAlester, Oklahoma, a small rural town that happened to be represented by Carl Albert, Speaker of the House. Another recipient was tiny Smithville, Tennessee, the hometown of powerful congressman Joe Evins, who was instrumental in getting the act passed and chaired the appropriations subcommittee with jurisdiction over funding.

What, then, was the point of the Model Cities program? As far as the problems of urban poverty and decay were concerned, *there was no point.* The task force had come up with a coherent, well-thought-out policy that was designed as an integrated whole to address these problems in an effective, innovative manner. But Congress destroyed the rational core of this policy, replacing it with a politically attractive substitute that made no intellectual sense and for which there was no credible justification. Indeed, the evisceration was actually begun by the task force itself, which was driven to corrupt its own ideas—by expanding the number of cities to sixty-six—simply because it knew that an intellectually sound program, concentrating money as it did on just a few cities, could not pass Congress.

Welcome to the good old days of congressional lawmaking. Many scholars, policymakers, and informed observers of American politics think wistfully about them and hope that, somehow, some way, the nation can bring them back. But the good old days are nothing we should aspire to resurrect. As the Model Cities program nicely illustrates, the history of congressional action is not a history of Congress assiduously providing coherent policy solutions to pressing social problems. Congress has often *reacted* to problems—but except in unusual circumstances, it has largely been incapable of crafting coherent policy solutions to them. Far more often, it has taken coherent ideas, ripped them apart, and reassembled them into cobbled-together packages that were literally *not designed* to achieve their loftily stated purposes. Strip away the many impediments to lawmaking in today's political world—the polarization, the narrow majorities, and those disruptive Tea Party members—and we are still left with a Congress that is fundamentally incapable of addressing the nation's vast array of serious problems.

BUILT-IN DEFICIENCIES

Congress can't be anything we want it to be. It is a constitutionally engineered institution, programmed to have certain features and behave in certain ways within the larger separation-of-powers system. Since the founding, the nation has been stuck with this increasingly archaic creation. To be sure, Congress has changed over the last two hundred years. It is no longer the dominion of party machines and spoils but a realm of entrepreneurial politicians with their own campaign organizations, their own support coalitions, their own sources of money. The fundamentals, however, have not changed. They are still there, ingrained in Congress's institutional genetics—and creating profound problems for the rest of American government.

These genetics are too often overlooked. Outside of academia, almost everyone who pays attention to Congress, and indeed to politics generally, tends to focus on the people involved—on John Boehner squaring off against Nancy Pelosi or Ted Cruz squaring off against everyone else. However natural this focus on newsworthy personalities may be, it is way off the mark. And misleading. The fact is, the specific people who make up Congress really don't matter all that much in the grand scheme of things. Get rid of the current crew of personalities and bring back that titan of the House, Tip O'Neill. Or another, Sam Rayburn. Or Wilbur Mills. Anybody you like. Or replace every single legislator with someone new. They will all be members of Congress, and they will all have their incentives and behavior shaped in very distinctive, common ways by the constitutionally prescribed nature of the institution (and its semi-prescribed electoral system). The people that make up Congress are easily observed. The structure that shapes their behavior is not. Yet it is precisely this structure that is fundamental.

A key to understanding Congress lies in recognizing that there are certain structural commonalities that explain why members do what they do, and thus what we can expect from them. Needless to say, these commonalities will not explain 100 percent of each member's behavior 100 percent of the time, but they do capture central tendencies—and those tendencies explain a lot of what happens in Congress. They get to the behavioral core of the institution. Three themes stand out.

Members of Congress are parochial. We've said it many times before, and we'll keep saying it. Congress is filled with political entrepreneurs, and they are constantly concerned about their own political welfare—which is rooted in the special interests, constituencies, and ideological support bases within their districts and states that make their reelections possible. It is no accident that Congress is awash in interest groups. All districts and states are inevitably made up of countless special interests; some, like banking or soybeans or automaking, vary enormously across districts while others, like senior citizens or veterans, are more evenly distributed—and members of Congress are wholly open to their lobbying activities and (selectively) responsive to their concerns and demands. The electoral connection is a two-way street: special interests seek influence while members of Congress seek popularity by being of service. It is also no accident that Congress is awash in money. This has always been true, but it is now true in the extreme thanks to recent Supreme Court decisions that have eviscerated campaign finance regulations. Members run their own campaigns and have an insatiable need for ever-greater sums to fill their electoral war chests, and the contributors are often key players who want special access in return. Again, it's a two-way street. For the most part, this is not a matter of corruption per se. The United States arguably has one of the cleanest political systems in the world (as political systems go). Such relationships are better understood in terms of mutuality of interest: a mutuality that favors rampant special-interest politics.[5]

To say that members of Congress are parochial is not to say that they are a bunch of country bumpkins. On the contrary, members of Congress tend to be quite cosmopolitan and well educated. Many have given up prestigious, lucrative jobs as lawyers, doctors, and businesspeople in order to serve. They are highly adept at doing what needs to be done to bolster and secure their local support. Theirs is an extraordinarily sophisticated parochialism. In office, they run complex media-relations operations that communicate with the press about pending legislation and advertise their achievements back home. With permanent support staff in both DC and their home districts, they shuttle back and forth for visits with key constituencies, interest groups, lobbying organizations, and fellow politicians. They work doggedly to secure set-asides of one kind or another—disaster relief, special contracts, earmarks, and other distributive outlays—for locally based companies and industries. They navigate a complex committee system that allows them to channel their professional ambitions by focusing on the bills that matter most to their constituents. Their résumés are impressive, their schedules are packed, and their operations are professional. They are high-performing reelection machines.

Members of Congress can be parochial, moreover, and still be ideological and have genuine interest in national and international issues. Their electoral fortunes may be tied, in part, to national economic trends, the president who sits in office, and national media.

Crises, particularly wars, may increase the salience of national considerations. In certain policy domains, notably those that are not especially salient to their constituents, members may have greater discretion in how they vote. And to fund their campaigns, members may call upon national interest groups and the support of their fellow partisans in Congress.[6]

Members are not exclusively parochial. But they are strongly influenced by parochial concerns. Nationalizing events and forces constitute deviations from a baseline that anchors them in localistic calculations and constraints. Their ideologies—which may seem to reflect broad political worldviews—must be in tune with their home-base ideological support constituencies, either because they are chosen on that basis or because they make ideological adjustments to bring themselves into local alignment. At every turn, they evaluate policy according to its local implications. They distribute their time and resources according to the demands of powerful interests from their districts and states. And nearly every word they say in every speech they give is drafted with an eye toward how it will play back home.

It is of no small relevance that, despite all the nationalizing forces of modern politics, members of Congress have increased the percentages of their own staff members working in their local offices rather than on Capitol Hill. In the Senate, the percentage of the senators' personal staff working in local offices rose from 25 percent in 1980 to 41 percent in 2010. In the House, the comparable figures were 34 percent and 49 percent. As these measures clearly suggest, members have hardly moved to distance themselves from parochial concerns over recent decades. They are tied to their states and districts. These are their political lifelines—and they invest their resources accordingly.[7]

Members of Congress are myopic. In addition to being parochial, legislators approach policy issues in shortsighted ways rather than being centrally concerned about the long-term consequences—or genuine effectiveness. House members are constantly running for reelection and are thus worried about the immediate impact of their decisions on constituents and interest groups. Senators have somewhat longer terms in office, but much the same is true for them. Among other things, members of Congress have strong incentives to fashion policies that provide current supporters with valuable up-front benefits, and they have strong incentives to push costs off into the future. This is why budget deficits, borrowing, and debt are so politically attractive—and such problems for the nation. It is also why Social Security and Medicare, the nation's two most expensive policy programs, are financial train wrecks waiting to happen: Congress is great at doling out benefits but terrible at requiring people to pay for them. These and other myopic pathologies are reinforced by the fact that, with 535 voting members in two chambers, individual legislators are not held responsible for the effectiveness of public policies, and there are no political consequences for them if policies turn out to be ineffective ten or twenty or thirty years down the road. Indeed, the incentives for members of Congress can actually work the other way around: if a policy turns out to be ineffective or even harmful, constituents can complain to their legislators, and legislators can get credit for riding to the rescue. As Morris Fiorina observed in his classic book *Congress: Keystone of the Washington Establishment*, members of Congress can actually benefit when policies don't work.[8]

Members of Congress think about the pieces, not the whole. This is an implication of their parochialism and myopia, really, but it's so important that it deserves separate emphasis. Members of Congress approach their policy decisions in a piecemeal fashion, focusing on just the policy in question—and the interest groups and constituents that want it—and not on how it fits into the nation's larger framework of policies, agencies, and governance. That is why, for example, a 2009 Government Accountability Office report found that the government had forty-seven different worker-training programs run by nine different federal agencies. Or why another study uncovered 82 programs to improve teacher quality, 160 to support housing, and 53 to promote entrepreneurship. Congress has devised no overarching, coherent national policy on worker training, teacher quality, housing, or entrepreneurship. Instead, it has produced a confusing, uncoordinated array of different programs adopted at different times for different reasons in response to different groups. Policies—and government—are constructed piece by piece, without any regard for crafting a well-functioning, rationally put-together whole. The same is true when Congress creates government agencies, assigns them missions, and locates them somewhere in the scheme of government. Upon its creation in 1964, for example, the food stamp program was handed over to the Department of Agriculture rather than the Department of Health, Education, and Welfare (now Health and Human Services, where almost all the nation's other social welfare programs were housed) because of a logroll aimed at getting the support of farm interests and Republicans. It has stayed there ever since, in odd and alien bureaucratic territory. There is no intellectual rhyme or reason to this sort of thing, no concern for building a coherent structure of government. The overall result is a governmental system characterized by duplication, overlap, and mismatch. It is an absolute mess—thanks, primarily, to the way members of Congress are wired to approach their jobs.[9]

PARTIES AND COMMITTEES ARE NO SOLUTION

So these are the basics. Members of Congress are shaped in common ways by the institutional genetics of the political system, and if they want to survive and prosper in that system, they have strong incentives to take an approach to policymaking that tends to be parochial, myopic, and piecemeal. They don't do these things because they are bad people. And they don't do them because, as human beings, they have little regard for good government or the national interest. They do them because, as political entrepreneurs, it is the rational way to behave. What we're seeing is an institutional phenomenon, not a personal one.

There is more to their behavior than just these basics, of course. Members are not just 535 disconnected individuals who do their own thing, separately pushing for their own advantage. For as they collectively operate within Congress, they are *organized* in very specific ways—and they need to be, because they must work together and cooperate to some degree if they are to get anything done, including bringing home the bacon to their own districts and states. After all, no one has an incentive to vote for anyone else's bacon, and majorities and agendas and compromises must be arranged if anything at all is to pass.

The way this is done is through parties and committees, which provide the internal organization of Congress and are the vehicles by which members actually make and influence policy. So it is reasonable to ask: do parties and committees somehow enable Congress to rise above the narrow perspectives of members to tackle the nation's policy problems in effective ways?

For the most part, the answer is no. Just as members are creatures of the institutional genetics of the system, so parties and committees are creatures of the members themselves—created by the members, for the members. Congress is internally organized in such a way as to allow the members to do a better, more effective job of advancing their own political welfare.

Committees allow members to specialize and develop expertise, which in turn enhances Congress's capacity to tackle more issues and get more work done. But the committee system also leads to a fragmentation and balkanization—and a proliferation of opportunities to block and delay—that allow members to carve out their own little bastions of power and privilege from which they can wring political advantage, provide benefits for constituents, do favors for powerful groups, and get money for campaigns. And they can do these things, needless to say, without crafting policies that are effective at solving the nation's problems.

What, then, about parties? Parties and the centralizing powers of their leaders would certainly seem to be Congress's best shot at addressing national issues in effective ways. Indeed, in recent decades, the parties have become ideologically polarized and party-line votes are very common. It may appear—John Boehner's 2015 resignation and the ensuing street fight for the House speakership notwithstanding—that party leaders have been strong enough to stifle the fractious inclinations of their members, coordinate and direct behavior, and make Congress into a coherent institutional decision-maker.

But they have not. Yes, there is a great deal of party-line voting. And some research shows that parties can occasionally discipline members' local orientations, at least when it comes to casting votes.[10] But it also is true that, in recent times, the constituencies within each party have become more homogeneous, mainly because the conservative South has gone Republican and the liberal

Northeast has become more Democratic. These shifts don't signal an abandonment of local constituencies or local ideological support bases. To the contrary, members of the nation's two parties have simply sorted themselves in ways that more coherently reflect broad geographic divisions within the country. The Republican Party is more rural, agrarian, religious, and conservative. The Democratic Party is more urban, industrial, secular, and liberal. The parties still reflect and represent local interests and the distinctive ideologies that go with them, but due to the sorting that has taken place, they do it in a different way than in decades past.[11]

As the parties have become more distant from one another and more internally homogeneous, party leaders—who are elected by the members and are highly sensitive to their local needs—have been better able to mobilize them to vote together. In part, this is because there are many more issues nowadays on which each party's members already agree. It is also because party members have something else of tangible importance—a "shared fate"—that further binds them together. Democrats are all affected by the electoral impact of their common Democrat label, and the same is true for Republicans. Within each party, then, there is a common concern for the party's reputation—and for allowing leaders to shape the party's policy agenda in electorally desirable ways and to corral votes in getting the agenda passed.[12]

Yet party members don't agree on everything regarding the substance of policy. Much of what looks like the power of leaders is really a reflection of shared constituency and electoral concerns. Except at the margins, leaders have no license to force members to do what they don't want to do—such as voting for gun control or free trade when their constituents at home are totally opposed. And for that matter, leaders have little incentive to use their powers that way, because they are elected by the members themselves, and because members need the flexibility to fend off local challengers, meet local imperatives, and represent their states and districts as they see fit. The leader's job—if the leader wants to stay a leader—is not to bludgeon members into voting with the party but rather to attract their support through trades and inducements designed to get them on board. These sorts of positive inducements are critical to building the necessary coalitions, but they also affect the details of policy, incorporating all manner of adjustments, compromises, and special-interest provisions to reflect the parochial concerns of the members who must be induced. In this way, parties can burnish their images and enhance their electoral prospects. But there is nothing about the coalitional process that requires the crafting of coherent, effective policy.[13]

Indeed, in many cases the very reason legislation can pass is that its intellectual integrity as a policy solution has been sacrificed along the way—or that it was never there to begin with. The Model Cities Act is a good example: Congress was able to pass a high-profile bill with a lofty-sounding name that claimed to address the problem of urban decay, but it didn't really attack that problem at all. Party leaders were able to marshal enough votes to get it through Congress precisely because it was *not* designed to solve the problem. Its ineffective design, in fact, was the key to its political success.

CONGRESS MAKES THE LAWS—BADLY

Many of the political scientists who study Congress for a living are very much taken with the institution and caught up in its details. They can recount the storied revolt against the powerful

Speaker Joe Cannon in 1910 and the subsequent empowerment of committee chairs. They can wax eloquent about the later frustration of northern liberals with southern Democrats' dominance of key committees, which led to the proliferation and power of subcommittees. And they can go on to describe in painstaking detail the later rise of polarized parties and the decline of cross-party coalitions. These and many other developments in the modern history of Congress are sources of endless fascination and study—and for good reason, for they are genuinely significant in helping to explain which policies pass and which don't, who has influence and who doesn't, and how these things have changed over time.

Through it all, however, the fundamentals have not changed. Congress is a parochial institution, and it has always been a parochial institution. That was perhaps okay two hundred years ago when times were simple and government wasn't expected to do much. But modern times are complex, demanding, and problem-filled in the extreme, and they call for a government capable of taking effective action. Which is precisely what Congress cannot do. It was never designed for such a formidable job, and today there should be no surprise that it is failing miserably at it. To be more specific:

1) Congress is often incapable of taking any action at all in response to pressing social problems, due to multiple opportunities for blocking by opposing interests.

2) When Congress does take action, its policies tend to be ineffective due to all the compromises, accommodations, and payoffs that are part of its parochial coalitional politics.

3) When its policies prove ineffective, Congress is typically unable to either fix them or get rid of them—and they often live on for decades.

We'll now elaborate on each point in turn.

Inaction in the Face of Serious Problems

Congress has passed untold thousands of laws over the years. Despite its fragmentation and multiple veto points, members have found ways to make things happen—which only makes sense given that it is by passing bills that members bring home benefits to their states and districts, carry the water for interest groups, and prove their worthiness for reelection. When it comes to major social problems, however, the complexities and stakes tend to be very high, powerful groups and constituencies are actively involved, and Congress's multiple veto points often prove insurmountable. The result is inaction. And problems that fester.

Take immigration. There are currently some eleven million undocumented immigrants in the country, most from Mexico and Latin America, who—whether some American citizens like it or not—have established lives here, are desperate to stay and work, but are living at the margins of society and suffering for it.[14] Donald Trump's campaign claims notwithstanding, eleven million people cannot be deported without massive cost, social unrest, and conflict. But nor can these undocumented people be ignored. Something needs to be done—maybe a path to citizenship, maybe something else, but *something*. In the meantime, the existing immigration law is not being enforced and the rule of law has become a joke. That is dangerous to our democracy and bad for everyone.

The nation clearly needs a law that can be enforced, upheld, and respected. It doesn't have one.

That's just one dimension of the problem. As any farmer in California can tell you, American agriculture depends heavily on immigrant labor to pick the crops that feed this nation (and the world). Yet the current law does not offer a workable arrangement, such as a truly effective guest worker program, that would enable that to happen. As a result, farmers are left in the lurch and harbor strong incentives to break the law and hire undocumented workers anyway. And then there's what might be called the Silicon Valley problem: existing laws make it very difficult for this country to attract talented, highly educated, highly skilled immigrants to fuel our business and technology sectors, even though it is clearly to the nation's advantage to open our doors to just these sorts of people. Other countries, such as Canada and Australia, have immigration laws that are strategically crafted for that purpose. Not ours. Ours does the opposite: it keeps high-value people out.[15]

These are long-standing issues of enormous significance to the nation, yet Congress has been hamstrung, unable to act. Serious reform efforts were led by Senators John McCain and Ted Kennedy (and supported by President George W. Bush) in 2005, 2006, and 2007—but the first failed in the House and the latter two failed on filibusters in the Senate. Why? Despite widespread public and business support for reform, various special interests found aspects they disagreed with. Social conservatives—the Republican base—fiercely objected to "amnesty." Farmers wanted more farmer-friendly provisions for seasonal workers than the reforms proposed. Asian and Latino groups wanted to keep the existing law's prioritization of family reunification. Latinos and liberals opposed stricter border enforcement. Unions wanted to protect their members from an influx of low-cost labor. And all these special interests had their congressional champions—who had veto points they could work. As the Brookings Institution's Darrell West astutely observed in an extensive study of immigration politics, Congress's inability to act is rooted in the nature of Congress itself: "The tendency for individual members of Congress to emphasize local concerns undermines consideration of broader and long-term national interests. . . . The combination of fragmented institutions, decentralized decision-making, localized politics, and an emotionally fraught issue has stymied comprehensive reform."[16]

For just these reasons, Congress tends to be immobilized on many other high-stakes issues as well. Consider health care. It is true, of course, that in 2010 President Obama succeeded in getting Congress to pass landmark legislation that significantly reformed the nation's health-care system. The backstory, however, is that presidents from both parties had been trying to bring about some form of universal health insurance *for sixty years*—with good reason—but consistently ran into a buzz saw of opposition in Congress, where special interests were able to block legislation. Obama's success is not the real headline here. Sixty years of blocking is.[17]

America's health-care system emerged haphazardly after World War II when larger firms, unable to attract workers through higher wages (due to wage-price controls), began offering their workers health benefits as a way of competing. Before long, employer-based health insurance became quite common—and it was subsidized at great expense by the government, which made such benefits tax deductible. By its nature, however, this approach left millions of Americans uninsured, it left millions more with inadequate or very costly coverage, and it created huge gaps and uncertainties for people who became unemployed or changed jobs. Nonetheless, the system was politically protected by businesses, unions, workers, insurance companies, hospitals, doctors, and many others who gained from it. And when presidents sought to bring some form of universal coverage to all Americans, they faced an entrenched opposition led by the American Medical Association (AMA), which denounced the expansion of coverage as "socialized medicine" and used its formidable leverage in Congress to block legislation.

Lyndon Johnson took advantage of his 1964 electoral landslide—and massive majorities in Congress—to push through Medicare and Medicaid. By American standards, these were major reforms. They extended coverage to the elderly and the poor. But they *only* extended coverage to the elderly and the poor—not to everyone—because Johnson had to scale back his ambitions in order to get any health-care reform at all through Congress's political minefield. At the end of the day, the employer-based system was left firmly in place, and millions of Americans remained uncovered or inadequately covered, leading many to be devastated by the costs of serious illness.

This system proved itself to be very, very ineffective as the decades wore on. As recent studies by the Commonwealth Fund, the *New England Journal of Medicine,* and the Organisation for Economic Co-operation and Development have shown, the United States' health-care system is the most costly and inefficient in the developed world. Americans spend about twice as much on health care, per capita, as the citizens of other developed countries do—and even so, our health-care outcomes are mediocre. Based on health-care criteria that include access, efficiency, equity, quality, and outcomes, the United States ranks dead last among the eleven nations studied (Australia, Canada, France, Germany, the Netherlands, New Zealand, Norway, Sweden, Switzerland, the United Kingdom, and the United States).[18]

This is what ineffectiveness looks like. The problems plaguing the American health-care system, moreover, have been apparent for decades. Obamacare was an attempt to deal with some of these problems. But putting that recent reform aside for the moment— we discuss it below—Congress has otherwise done nothing during these many decades to craft a coherent policy solution that would give the nation a well-integrated, well-functioning system that can produce high-quality health outcomes at reasonable prices. Is this too much to ask? Apparently so, but only because special interests with a stake in the traditional employer-based system have tremendous influence in Congress, and they have found ways to block anything that is truly broad, coherent, and cost-efficient.

Ineffectiveness by Design

Although often immobilized on issues of genuine import, legislators still need to take action in order to demonstrate their political value to constituents. So Congress still manages to crank out lots of legislation. The nation, in fact, is buried in it. And inevitably, the ostensible purpose of virtually every piece of legislation is to address some sort of social problem—even if it involves building a "bridge to nowhere" intended to benefit a handful of people (as well as construction companies and their workers) in Alaska. Members of Congress are often happy to pass laws—but there is a big difference between passing laws and solving social problems.

So when Congress does act, what does its legislation tend to look like? The answer is not that it somehow rises above the special interests and parochial pressures but rather that it pieces together legislative products that accommodate and cater to them. Such is the prerequisite for building a sufficiently large coalition across two houses and multiple veto points in order to get something passed. That something, however, is likely to be a patchwork creation rather than a genuine solution to a social problem.

As we've seen, the Model Cities Act is a good example of how the special-interest compromises necessary to build a coalition also undermine the coherence of legislation. But the Affordable Care Act (ACA)—Obamacare—is another good example and a much more consequential one, for this was a landmark piece of legislation. What Obama achieved here, in getting a more expansive health insurance bill through Congress, was truly historic. He overcame great political odds and powerful vested interests that had stifled other modern presidents—Truman, Kennedy, Johnson, Nixon, Ford, Carter, Clinton—who had sought much the same goal for more than half a century. But in American politics, success is relative. Obama settled for much less than he wanted. More to the point: he settled for a new "system" that had Congress's parochial fingerprints all over it.

Obama had little choice. Knowing that Bill Clinton had gone down in flames in 1994 trying to push his own version of universal health insurance on a resistant Congress, the president resolved to be pragmatic and give Congress much greater scope to design a new system it could embrace. He would provide leadership, guidance, and ideas, but it would be up to Congress to craft something that would greatly expand coverage—and attract enough votes to pass, which meant that powerful interests would need to be accommodated. Most ideas for crafting a coherent approach to the problem would have to be scrapped or compromised.[19]

The insurance companies and conservatives defeated the "public option," which would have allowed the government to offer competing insurance policies as one means of keeping prices down. They also defeated the single-payer option of end-running insurance companies and making government the insurer. The pharmaceutical companies prevented Americans from gaining the right to buy prescription drugs from Canada and from having any protection from the astronomical drug prices they had been paying—prices much, much higher than those paid by citizens in other countries. The trial lawyers headed off tort reforms that would have limited doctors' malpractice liabilities and crushing insurance premiums, another means of trying to moderate prices. And so on. One special-interest victory after another, in a bill that is more than a thousand pages long. And through it all, the sundry vested interests that supported the traditional employer-based system continued to hold sway—ensuring that the old system would remain right at the core of American health-care policy and that the old providers would gain millions of new customers. The new system would essentially consist of new components grafted onto the old, despite its perversities, resulting in an incredibly complex patchwork that no one would have favored or designed if working from the ground up—and that never seriously tackled the critical challenge of reducing health-care costs. This is what "system reform" looks like when Congress is in the driver's seat.

The ACA isn't the only cobbled-together patchwork that denies the country genuine reform. Consider tax policy. Tax policy has far-reaching implications for economic growth, incentives to invest and consume, issues of inequality and poverty, and much more. Any nation that seeks to promote the economic and social well-being of its citizens needs to have a rational fiscal policy designed with these ends in mind. And a rational tax policy is absolutely essential if that is to be possible. Governments cannot spend and tax in whatever ways they want and think the outcomes for society will be good. They need a coherent, well-thought-out policy.

The United States can't have one. Presidents have tried, through the Council of Economic Advisers, the US Department of the Treasury, and other means. But the taxing power is vested in Congress, and its members have used it to serve the special interests of their states and districts and do favors for powerful groups. For parochial politicians, making tax policy is the ultimate political bonanza. It gives them the capacity to be individually helpful in doling out specialized benefits to anyone, any group, any firm, and any industry they want—often so buried in the complex tax code that no one else even knows they are there—and without having to create a fiscal whole that makes any kind of intellectual sense.

In 1913, passage of the Sixteenth Amendment authorized the income tax and laid the groundwork for the modern tax system. The same year, Congress enacted the first significant tax break for oil companies, the "oil depletion allowance." Soon thereafter, with the end of World War I, Washington was swarming with business interests determined to take advantage of Congress's new powers. Interest groups with names like the Business Men's National Tax Committee, the Farmers' Federal Tax League, and the National Association of Retailers agitated against higher wartime taxes— necessary to fund the war—and battled each other over various sales tax proposals and tax breaks. Among all interest groups, the oil and gas industries did especially well.[20]

The structure of Congress and the susceptibility of its members to special-interest lobbying eventually led to a byzantine tax code that was rife with giveaways to organized interests. In the second half of the twentieth century, as government became much bigger and more active, Congress only magnified these developments by its frequent reliance on "tax expenditures" to fund its social policies. By giving firms and individuals targeted tax breaks, Congress

could promote particular policy objectives, such as home ownership or investment in solar energy or new sources of oil, without
adding to the federal budget or requiring additional agencies or
personnel. As a means of doling out benefits to interest groups and
constituents, these uses of the tax code were politically ideal. They
involved no up-front expense, created no immediate losers, and
spread the costs (which were essentially hidden) across the public
at large.

With the tax code an obvious monstrosity, there have been pe-
riodic efforts—led by presidents—to bring about major reform by
making the code much simpler, fairer, and more coherent. The last
and most successful of all tax reforms was the Tax Reform Act of
1986, during the Reagan presidency, which stripped away literally
thousands of special-interest tax breaks—with great political pain
and anguish all around—and produced a much-improved tax
code. Even so, it also contained hundreds of instances in which the
law was purposely built to favor particular industries or legislative
districts, and more than seven hundred "transition rules" were
written into the law that exempted certain powerful entities, including Pan Am Airways, from being affected by the changes. In
one case, the law targeted benefits to a single taxpayer, in this case
an oil heiress who resided in the Speaker of the House's congressional district. Overall, the cost of such special rules in the 1986
act was estimated at $10.6 billion.[21]

The achievements of the 1986 reform, moreover, were only
temporary. Tax decisions were still in the hands of Congress, and
the political incentives of its members were exactly the same as
always. In the following years, the simplicity and coherence of the
new tax code were corrupted again and again as Congress went
about its normal business of incrementally adding special-interest

privileges for interests ranging from NASCAR drivers to Native American whaling operations. By 2005, a panel appointed by President George W. Bush counted fifteen thousand addendums to the tax code since 1986.[22] Less than twenty years after its passage, the most far-reaching tax reform package of all time had been entirely overthrown and parochialized. Death by fifteen thousand cuts.

The United States has a tax policy that doesn't even deserve to be called a policy. While corporations and lobbyists manipulate the code for their own benefit, ordinary people have no idea what's in it, and even sophisticated observers of politics don't remotely understand it. It's too complicated, too convoluted—and too long. Indeed, the current tax code is so long that a debate has broken out over exactly how long it is. By one estimate, it is upwards of seventy thousand pages. By another it is about 2,600 pages. No one knows for sure. Whatever its true length, it is doubtless the most complex tax code in the developed world. And it is a special-interest travesty, perhaps the purest reflection of what Congress naturally does when it gets its hands on economic policy.[23]

Congress's tendency to parochialize policy, however, knows no bounds, and it happens in realms where most people would never expect it. We've already seen how Congress is incapable of addressing big, salient issues like immigration and universal health care, and we've seen how tax policy is a special-interest playground. But what about policies that would seem to be nonpolitical and that deal with "easy" matters that lend themselves to straightforward public-interest legislation? What about, say, school lunches?

Buckle up. In the wake of America's experience with widespread poverty and deprivation during the Great Depression, nutrition experts and social-welfare advocates made a strong case that children, especially low-income children, were in need of nutritious meals if they were to grow up healthy and make the most of their time in school. Congress responded in 1946 with the National School Lunch Program. This program is still with us, subsidizing some thirty-one million lunches every school day at an annual cost of roughly $11.6 billion.[24] After food stamps, the school lunch program is the federal government's largest food program.

But the nation's school lunch program isn't just about helping kids. Its key designer in 1946 was Senator Richard Russell, whose home state of Georgia was overwhelmingly rural and agricultural. With support from other southern Democrats, along with other members of Congress from agricultural areas, Russel crafted a program that would simultaneously provide lunches to needy kids *and* provide an outlet for surplus agricultural products that were being purchased by the federal government under Depression-era programs to prop up farm incomes. Russell and his supporters specified, moreover, that the lunch program would be administered and controlled by the Department of Agriculture. Such a design was a politically compelling combination that provided the coalition of strange bedfellows necessary for Congress to pass the legislation.[25]

The 1946 law also, and with great consequence, linked the school lunch program to a vast array of powerful agricultural interests. This connection only grew stronger as the program and its funding expanded over the next few decades, and school lunches became a giant, highly profitable new market for all manner of food products, from potatoes to peanuts to pizza. Firms and industry groups lobbied heavily to get their products on the menu. They were not in the business of providing the most nutritious meals possible for poor kids. They were in the business of making money and selling whatever products they could. They were also very powerful within Congress and the Department of Agriculture. And the department's mission, after all, is to promote the interests of American farmers—it is not a social welfare agency. The designers were well aware of that.

Since its original enactment, the National School Lunch Program has been revised various times, but meeting the seemingly simple goals of providing nutritious food and serving needy kids has proven to be a constant, unwinnable struggle. Agricultural and corporate power are stacked against it. Southern Democrats in the 1940s and 1950s wanted the money for their districts and their farmers, but they did not want that money to go to African American schools and children, and they did not want to give the federal government any power to set eligibility rules that would allow the feds to interfere with the Jim Crow customs that then prevailed. Although Representative Adam Clayton Powell was successful in attaching a nondiscrimination amendment to the 1946 bill, that provision was not enforced by the Department of Agriculture. And until the 1960s, when liberals rewrote the rules, the National School Lunch Program rarely served black children; indeed, it mainly served a clientele of middle-class white kids. Only in the late 1960s—and especially with a major expansion under Richard Nixon, who aimed to ensure that poor kids got their lunches totally free—did the program really get serious about providing lunches to needy kids. It took about twenty-five years for that to happen.

In the decades since, free and reduced-price lunch has become a pervasive part of American schooling, but it remains only partially successful.[26] Sometimes poor kids go unserved. But the big lingering problem is nutrition, which suffers because unhealthy food is often cheaper for school districts to buy, and the powerful food interests are only too happy to provide it. With obesity a critical national problem—roughly a third of all American kids are now obese or overweight and thus at risk later in life for diabetes, stroke, heart disease, and more—there is much public support for better nutrition. And with Michelle Obama taking the lead, Congress passed (with much opposition in the House) the Healthy, Hunger-Free Kids Act of 2010, which made notable upgrades to decades-old nutrition standards for school lunches. But the Department of Agriculture is still in charge of the regulations, there are still many members of Congress speaking for food companies and agribusinesses, and every step toward better nutrition is a battle.

Take an "issue" so apparently simple as pizza sauce. Almost all Americans, we hazard to guess, would be surprised to hear that pizza sauce is a source of big-time political controversy. But it is. Because in the last few years, the Department of Agriculture changed its rule about how the nutritional value of tomato paste would be assessed, and that change yielded a much lower nutritional value for pizza, threatening its place on the menu. That, in turn, brought immediate blowback from the Schwan Food Company, a Minnesota-based food giant—fourteen thousand employees, some $3 billion in annual sales—that supplies 70 percent of all the pizza served in America's schools.[27] Schwan and its allies formed the Coalition for Sustainable School Meal Programs to lobby against this and other objectionable rules (for example, one discriminating against potatoes). Representative Collin Peterson, a centrist Democrat whose Minnesota district is where Schwan's headquarters is located, dutifully threatened to insert a rider into the department's budget bill to block implementation of the tomato paste rule. Senator Amy Klobuchar, also a Democrat from Minnesota, went to bat for Schwan in her own chamber, bringing many Democrats along. In the end, the rider passed, blocking the tomato rule (and the potato rule too).

We could go on, but you get the point. Nutritious lunches for needy children? As simple as that sounds—and ought to be—Congress just isn't up to the challenge. And it hasn't been for over seventy years.

The Protected Lives of Ineffective Laws

So far we've discussed two ways in which Congress is profoundly deficient as the nation's lawmaker. The first is that, especially when faced with social problems of great importance, it often cannot act—for decades—and the problems persist. The second is that, when it does take action, it tends to fashion parochial, cobbled-together laws that aren't even designed to effectively address the problems at hand.

These are serious deficiencies. But there's more. In any governmental system, not just our own, it's likely that even the most serious, public-spirited efforts to devise policy solutions to social problems will turn out, with experience, to need adjustment. There are bound to be mistakes and glitches of various types. Or unintended consequences. Or theories and expectations that, while entirely reasonable at the outset, turn out to be wide of the mark. Or societal changes that no one anticipated. Precisely for these sorts of reasons, good policymaking can't be a one-shot deal. It has to be a *process* in which policies are evaluated in light of experience and adaptations are made to fix whatever might be wrong and promote better outcomes. These fixes may involve, most obviously, changes to the policy itself. But in some cases—indeed many cases, if the time period is long enough—experience may suggest that the policy is no longer needed (or that it never was, or is too flawed to fix) and that it should be removed from the books. Laws become outmoded, especially in a dynamic society, and they often need to go.

Congress is very bad at these adaptive adjustments. Outmoded, ineffective, and often expensive laws remain on the books for years when there is no justification for them. And policies that experience has shown are flawed and in need of fixes are nonetheless not fixed, or not fixed well, but are allowed to live on in their flawed form, soaking up resources that could be much better spent elsewhere.[28]

The corpus of Congress-made laws is filled with examples of both types of adaptive failures. An illuminating illustration of the first is the nation's experience with the Merchant Marine Act, also known as the Jones Act, which was adopted in 1920. The act requires that all goods shipped between US ports (including territories like Puerto Rico and Guam) be transported on US-made ships that are manned by US crews. The stated purpose was to help the government sell off its large fleet of merchant ships after World War I and also—as a sheer act of protectionism—to promote the US shipping industry. It was also a brilliant exercise in political entrepreneurialism by one Wesley Jones, a Republican senator from the state of Washington, who steered the law through Congress—and thereby ensured that Alaska would become dependent on Seattle-based ships for its many shipping needs.[29]

Almost one hundred years later, the Jones Act is still the law of the land. Yet there is no good justification for it, it jacks up the cost of shipping, and we all pay those unnecessary costs year after year after year. A report by the Federal Reserve Bank of New York indicates that it costs about $3,000 to ship a twenty-foot container from the East Coast of the United States to Puerto Rico, but the same shipment can be sent to the nearby Dominican Republic (not a US territory) for about $1,500. If the act were repealed, commercial ships from all over the world could compete to haul cargo from one part of America to another. This would lower prices. It would especially lower them for the transport of oil, which experts estimate foreign-flagged ships could transport for one-third of the cost of US-flagged ships.[30]

Why, then, does the Jones Act stay in place? The reasons have precious little to do with the public interest. Legislators from states and districts connected to the shipbuilding industry face pressure from their constituents to keep things as they are. This shipping coalition—made up of shipping companies plus the Maritime Trades Department of the AFL-CIO, the International Longshore and Warehouse Union, the Sailors' Union of the Pacific, and other labor groups—use their political leverage with Congress to oppose anything that looks like reform.[31] And there are many ways to block. Between 1995 and 2000, four bills were introduced to repeal the act, and three additional bills were introduced to amend its construction and ownership provisions—but none even made it out of committee. In 2010, Senators John McCain (R-AZ) and Jim Risch (R-ID) introduced the Open America's Waters Act, a bill to repeal the Jones Act—but again, that bill was buried in committee. In 2015, John McCain introduced yet another proposal for repeal, but so far (no surprise) it is languishing. Decades of reform attempts, then, have come up short. The Jones Act lives on, approaching its one hundredth birthday—an expensive, unjustified exercise in protectionism that Congress has been unable to eliminate.

The kind of thing that happened with the Jones Act happens regularly across all realms of public policy. When government adopts new programs, there are typically constituencies and interest groups that benefit from what those programs do—from the spending, the contracts, the jobs, the favorable rules. And should the programs come under attack later on for being unnecessary or overly costly or ineffective, the beneficiary groups—which now have strong vested interests in these particular niches of government—can be counted upon to bring their political power to bear with Congress in order to obstruct change. Sometimes they can block it. Sometimes they can just stifle, weaken, and distort it. Either way, government becomes laden with programs that don't work very well, don't ever get fixed, and don't go away.[32]

Consider the nation's key farm programs, which were adopted during the New Deal but are still with us, like a heavy yoke around our necks. The 1930s, of course, was a time of desperation and poverty for America's farmers, and Franklin Roosevelt was committed to remedying the situation. His plan, enacted by a supportive Congress, involved paying subsidies to farmers for growing certain crops—corn, wheat, soybeans, sugar, peanuts, and much more, the amount of the subsidy varying with the type of crop and market conditions—as well as various mechanisms, ranging from market quotas to simply paying farmers not to plant their fields. The aim was to provide a safety net for American farmers by propping up their incomes, controlling supply, and protecting them from the operation of market forces.

With the rise of economic prosperity in the decades following World War II, the plight of farmers improved. No longer did they live in the era of John Steinbeck's *Grapes of Wrath*. The weight of expert opinion among economists, moreover, was that the New Deal programs were inefficient, distorted the allocation of resources, and were bad policy. Presidents from both parties agreed, as did many market-oriented Republicans. But the farm sector became much better organized for political action as specialized interest groups emerged to represent virtually every commodity, and these groups used their considerable power in Congress, particularly with members of the agriculture committees, to ensure that the New Deal subsidy and acreage allotment programs lived on.[33]

Through a logroll between urban legislators, who agreed to vote for the farm programs, and rural legislators, who agreed to vote for food stamps for the disadvantaged, the New Deal farm programs did indeed live on. In the meantime, the family farm was becoming extinct, and virtually all the benefits of the subsidies and allotment payments were going to huge agribusinesses. The whole New Deal system, originally aimed at protecting the family farm, had become a deeply entrenched system of corporate welfare—one that few experts could support as being in the best interests of the nation. By the late 1980s, almost 25 percent of the farm acreage for major crops was lying fallow. And as a study by economist Bruce Gardner showed, the system was transferring almost $18 billion from taxpayers to (big) farmers, and consumers were paying some $5 billion in higher commodity prices than they otherwise would. A net negative for society—with ordinary people paying the costs.[34]

As part of the Gingrich "Contract with America" revolt in the late 1990s, Republicans succeeded in passing the Federal Agriculture Improvement and Reform Act in 1996, which eliminated most subsidies, did away with acreage limitations, and made the reform easier on agribusinesses by allowing them to receive massive transition payments over a period of seven years. But then crop prices tanked, the farming sector screamed for help, and Congress caved. The transition payments were so greatly enhanced that, by 2000, literally half of all farm income was coming from taxpayers. And in 2002, after a bidding war between Democrats and Republicans to please farm interests, Congress adopted a new farm bill that reinstated the crop subsidies—but at higher levels than before, with a new subsidy program for dairy farmers, and at a total cost billions of dollars higher than if the earlier program had just been continued.[35]

The New Deal farm subsidy programs were designed roughly eighty years ago to help the distressed family farmer. Today, American agriculture is dramatically different—far more prosperous, far more technologically advanced, run by giant agribusinesses. Yet these archaic programs are still with us, embedded in the structure of government and law. They are inefficient. They impose costs on consumers and taxpayers while funneling money into corporate coffers. Yet they survive because Congress protects them, can't fix them, and won't let them die.[36]

The nation's long and troubled experience with its key welfare program, Aid to Families with Dependent Children (AFDC), offers yet another illustration. This program too originated in the New Deal, enacted as part of the Social Security Act of 1935 to provide financial support for children of destitute widows. It was later expanded to provide payments more generally for children who did not have fathers in the home, with money thus going to women in poverty who were unmarried, divorced, or separated. (Much later, two-parent households received support as well, but single mothers continued to receive greater benefits.)

In the 1960s, with the elections of John F. Kennedy and Lyndon Johnson, the publication of Michael Harrington's seminal study of poverty, *The Other America*, and the launching of Johnson's War on Poverty and Great Society, poverty became a high-salience issue for the nation. Even many conservatives agreed that the federal government needed to take action to mitigate the problem. It was widely recognized, however, that the country's core program to combat poverty, AFDC, had serious flaws and was very ineffective.[37]

Beyond the usual partisan conflicts over welfare—with liberals and their allies wanting more support, better opportunities, and more respect for the poor, and conservatives worried about excessive costs, waste, and abuse—there were broader, more general problems with AFDC as a program that crossed familiar partisan lines. Among other things, the very design of AFDC gave women less incentive to marry and stay married, and indeed gave young, poor, single women more incentive to have kids out of wedlock as a means of getting welfare payments. It encouraged the breakup of families and, with poverty so high among blacks, was especially threatening to black families. And it reduced the incentive to work and threatened an unending cycle of dependence that was ultimately good for no one—not for the poor, not for society.

Liberals and conservatives agreed that AFDC was badly designed, didn't work, and needed to be fixed. They disagreed on how to fix it. And as policy solutions were proposed and pursued over the decades, Congress was a battleground in which legislators and diverse interest groups on both sides—including civil rights groups, the National Welfare Rights Organization, Americans for Democratic Action, assorted church groups, the US Chamber of Commerce, the National Association of Manufacturers, and many, many more—fought over the various proposals. The most serious effort to create a coherent new approach to welfare came from President Richard Nixon, whose proposal, the Family Assistance Plan (FAP), was crafted by adviser (later senator) Daniel Moynihan, a Democrat. The proposal was based on economist Milton Friedman's idea of a negative income tax, which was intended to provide guaranteed income support for all needy people, whether working or nonworking, and do away with the focus on unwed mothers.

But here again, the congressional battleground proved to be a graveyard. Nixon's Family Assistance Plan had a lot going for it— it was a serious, truly innovative attempt to fix the nation's failed welfare system through comprehensive reform, championed by a Republican president no less. But while FAP had plenty of support- ers, there were too many powerful groups with their own dispa- rate, dissenting ideas about what a new policy should look like. Some on the left—including the National Welfare Rights Organi- zation, which represented AFDC recipients—thought FAP didn't provide sufficiently high payments, imposed racist and punishing work requirements, and favored men over women. Some business and conservative groups—including the Chamber of Commerce, which made defeating FAP its number-one priority—saw the plan as too costly and thought it weakened incentives to work. The Nixon coalition succeeded in getting FAP passed by the House but ran into a wall in the Senate. The bill was controlled by the Senate Finance Committee, which was chaired by Richard Long of Loui- siana and heavily populated by conservatives from rural, non-northern areas. With the unusual help of liberal opponents, the committee eviscerated and ultimately blocked the bill. It never made it out onto the Senate floor—where the Nixon people esti- mated that it had some sixty votes—and died a very normal con- gressional death.

Several years later, with the AFDC program still justifiably in the crosshairs, President Jimmy Carter pursued a welfare reform proposal that picked up the main components of Nixon's Family Assistance Plan. The fact that Carter and Nixon were from differ- ent parties made little difference. Indeed, Carter's program was even more comprehensive, seeking to consolidate the nation's piecemeal attempts at support for the poor—not just through AFDC but also through food stamps, the Supplemental Security Program (SSI, adopted in 1974), the Earned Income Tax Credit (EITC, adopted in 1975), and Section 8 housing vouchers (adopted in 1974)—into one coherent welfare policy. But here again, there were interest groups on both the left and the right that took issue with Carter's plan, albeit for very different reasons. And to make matters worse, the new piecemeal welfare enactments during the 1970s—SSI, EITC, Section 8—had created new constituencies that did not want their benefits changed or threatened by a comprehensive reform of welfare. So Carter's plan, too, went down to defeat. It never got out of committee.[38]

Meantime, AFDC lived on with all its manifest flaws—and it continued to be a matter of high salience in American public policy. As political scientist Lawrence Mead observed in 1992, "Since the 1960s, the leading question in social politics has been how to reform AFDC so as to minimize dependency by people who many feel could support themselves." Efforts to achieve major reform soldiered on. And they met with little success for many frustrating years, until finally in 1996 the political stars happened to line up— when Bill Clinton, having pledged in his 1992 campaign to "end welfare as we have come to know it" and facing political irrelevance with the Republican takeover of Congress in 1995, joined forces with Gingrich Republicans to pass a major reform bill to replace AFDC. The Temporary Assistance for Needy Families (TANF) program, which made assistance temporary and instituted work requirements, has since been regarded by many experts—but by no means all—as a success. That is saying a lot. Yet TANF does not even attempt to accomplish the kind of comprehensive reform that Nixon, Carter, and others had envisioned earlier. Instead, it adds one more component to the nation's myriad piecemeal, uncoordinated programs to aid the poor. SSI, EITC, Section 8, and food stamps are all still out there, each functioning on its own. And as of 1996, TANF has joined them. This is America's welfare "policy."[39]

The point to be emphasized here is not that TANF falls short. It is that the AFDC program was clearly very deficient, liberals and conservatives alike were acutely aware of its problems, and yet Congress kept AFDC in place for a full sixty years without being able to fix it. This, moreover, is business as usual. Bad policies live for a long, long time even when everyone knows they are bad.

Finally, we think it is instructive to take a look at a flawed policy of rather recent vintage—No Child Left Behind (NCLB)—that Congress actually did take "quick" action to fix (or so it would appear), passing major new legislation in late 2015. On the surface, Congress's handling of NCLB might seem to be an example of responsible governance. But that is precisely why it is worth discussing, because a look at what happened reveals the same pathologies that we've been seeing all along.

NCLB was adopted by Congress in 2001. It was a landmark piece of legislation that sought to significantly improve the American education system—and thus, to address the nation's vexing problem of low student achievement—by holding states, school districts, and public schools accountable for teaching children what they need to know. Normally, such watershed legislation would never have passed. But it was a top priority of the new president, George W. Bush, who had been a champion of school accountability as governor of Texas; Republicans in Congress were willing to support their new president, and also to steal the education issue from Democrats; key Democrats (like Ted Kennedy) were willing to go along out of frustration with the failures of urban education reform, and also to prevent Republicans from gaining an edge on education; and minority groups, long opposed to testing, switched sides to become big supporters. For one shining moment, there was a coalition for major change—and NCLB became law.[40]

In scope, comprehensiveness, and sheer ambition, NCLB was unprecedented. It created a common system of accountability for America's schools—seeking to improve the quality of education for all students in the nation, but particularly for the disadvantaged, who had long suffered from what President Bush called the "soft bigotry of low expectations." What it did, in simple terms, was to institute a regime of annual testing, require that all schools be evaluated every year on whether they had made "adequate yearly progress," and set out consequences for schools that failed to do so. But to make such a system of accountability work, and work well, was an enormously complex undertaking and entirely new for the federal government. This was exactly the kind of situation that called for an ongoing process of learning, adaptation, and adjustment. But that, of course, is precisely what American government cannot do.

NCLB was afflicted by two big problems. First, it was poorly designed. Among other things, the way it measured "adequate yearly progress" was flawed, so school performance was not being reliably assessed; indeed, many schools were classified—very publicly—as failing when they really weren't. So the legislation clearly needed to be fixed. The second problem was political. Soon after NCLB's adoption, the powerful teachers unions went on the warpath to bring it down, launching media campaigns against "over testing" to convince Americans that NCLB was bad policy (a strategy much aided by NCLB's very real flaws) and putting relentless pressure on Democrats to overturn it. In the meantime, rightward-moving Republicans were abandoning ship. In 2001, many had violated their commitment to local control in order to support their president's signature legislation. But as the years passed, and with the Tea Party brewing, they closed ranks against what they now called "federal overreach."[41]

The results proved bizarre even by American standards. Democrats and Republicans both heaped their own criticisms on NCLB. Yet although many agreed that it suffered from flaws that were correctible, fixing them turned out to be impossible. NCLB was scheduled to come up for reauthorization in 2007, which was the obvious opportunity for revision and adjustment. But 2007 came and went, with Congress totally gridlocked by the diversity of views among supporters and opponents as to what should be done. So nothing was done. NCLB lived on for another eight agonizing years—screaming out for revision, but encased in legislative concrete as it was originally written.

Meantime, President Obama was stuck with implementing a very flawed and much-vilified law, and he chose under the circumstances not to fully enforce its provisions. Instead, in 2012 he began granting the states waivers using criteria that encouraged them to pursue certain reforms—among them, performance-based evaluations of teachers and Common Core national standards—that were favored by his administration *but not actually part of NCLB at all*. Throughout most of Obama's second term in office, then, the nation's accountability policy was made through presidential discretion, not through congressional legislation. NCLB remained on the books, but it was not really the law. It was a zombie statute.[42]

When the Republicans assumed control of Congress in 2015, they took aim at NCLB. By acting in a de facto alliance with their arch enemies, the teachers unions, whose power brought many Democrats along, Republicans passed the Every Student Succeeds Act (ESSA) in December 2015. Under the new law, students would still be tested annually and the results made public. But actual accountability—including what the academic standards would be, how performance would be measured, how schools would be evaluated, and what consequences (if any) would be imposed on those that were failing—would now be in the discretionary hands of state and local governments.

As is par for the course, the ESSA was heralded in Congress with much lofty language. Said Senator Lamar Alexander (R-TN), the act's key architect, the ESSA "will unleash a flood of excitement and innovation and student achievement that we haven't seen in a long time. But it will come community by community, state by state, rather than through Washington, D.C."[43] Such expectations are wildly optimistic. The reality is that the teachers unions and the school districts do not want schools, teachers, or districts held accountable for their performance, and they are far more powerful at lower levels of government than they are at the national level. Resistance to accountability will not stop just because the federal government is pushed to the sidelines. The resistance will continue, and with even greater leverage.[44]

The point we want to make here, however, is not that ESSA is worse than the flawed NCLB. It is new, and time will tell. The point is that, for some fourteen years, the nation and its public school system suffered at the hands of a hugely consequential piece of legislation that by everyone's account desperately needed to be fixed, yet Congress did nothing to fix it. There was no excuse for putting the nation through so much confusion and disorganization. Congress's behavior was irresponsible. It was costly. It was harmful. And when Congress finally mobilized itself to take action, it essentially just punted—taking the nation back to a status quo ante that had never worked well to begin with, and refusing to seriously address the nation's longstanding problem of weak educational performance.

A Systemic Mess

We have focused here on the content of laws and the politics behind them, and we've done that for a good reason. Laws are fundamental. They are the primary means by which government acts. Under the Constitution, Congress is granted the authority to make the laws, and the fact that it makes them badly—and indeed, is *wired* to make them badly—fatally undermines the ability of American government to meet the challenges of modern society.

We could stop our critique right here, because it gets to the heart of the matter. Yet we need to emphasize that the constitutionally based pathologies that afflict Congress have an array of consequences that go well beyond the laws themselves. They profoundly shape—and distort and undermine—the entire governmental system that is given the responsibility for carrying out those laws. In overseeing the government, Congress has crafted a system in its own image.

The Bureaucracy

In assessing their situation at the turn of the twentieth century, the Progressives were right about most of the things that counted—including their recognition that a strong, coherent bureaucracy is a hallmark of modern government. But they were wrong in thinking that there could be a "separation of politics from administration" and that this would allow professionalism, expertise, coherence, and rationality to prevail. What they didn't know was that, in the American constitutional system, such a separation is impossible, at least as a general matter. It was impossible then, and it is impossible now. The bureaucracy is the product of politics—and thoroughly politicized.[45]

The agencies and departments of the federal bureaucracy are created and organized by Congress, are overseen by Congress, receive their programs and funding from Congress, and are thoroughly enmeshed in congressional politics. Members of Congress don't just enact policies and hand them over to an objective, professional bureaucracy for implementation. That's not what legislators want. They see the bureaucracy as an extension of the policy process. Just as they want to craft, manipulate, and control policy for their own parochial ends, so they want to do exactly the same to the bureaucracy—because it is in the bureaucracy that policy will become real and interest groups and constituencies will or will not get what they want.

When members make decisions about specific policies, then, they also make decisions about specific pieces of the bureaucracy. Each piece is a separately conceived and orchestrated political product, fashioned by a unique coalition of legislators and interest groups that have the votes—right then, at the time—to promote a particular set of interests. How they do that, moreover, is highly strategic and reflects a "politics of structure" that is very much like the politics of policymaking. Members have incentives to layer new programs onto the old (which can't be gotten rid of) and to locate them in different parts of the bureaucracy with their own rules, funding, and distinctive status—leading, as we've seen, to countless numbers of worker training programs, teacher quality programs, and the like and, more generally, to rampant duplication, overlap, and organizational messiness. We've also seen that members have incentives to put their agencies and programs in friendly departments—which farm groups and legislators did in demanding that the food stamps and school lunch programs become part of the Department of Agriculture bureaucracy. And in a further attempt to insulate their favorite programs, members may bury agencies in restrictive formal rules that sharply reduce bureaucratic discretion and specify exactly what agencies must do. The resulting "overbureaucratization" hurts an agency's capacity for using its expertise and professional judgment, which further erodes the government's ability to effectively solve problems.[46]

In a system that makes the blocking of legislation and reform easy, moreover, policy supporters aren't the only ones involved in decisions about bureaucracy. A policy's political enemies may get to play some sort of role if any legislation is to pass—and they may insist, as part of the toll they exact, on getting to design some of the bureaucratic pieces. When the Occupational Safety and Health Administration (OSHA) was first created, for example, business groups that opposed it were powerful enough to demand just such a toll. Labor unions and their supporters wanted a single, centralized regulatory agency for occupational safety and health, located in the friendly Department of Labor. But business used its power to insist upon—and win—a highly fragmented, internally divided structure fully intended to weaken regulation and destroy its coherence. Yes, there would be an OSHA within the Department of Labor. But there would also be an entirely separate, independent agency, the Occupational Safety and Health Review Commission, with the authority to review and overturn OSHA's enforcement decisions. There would be yet another agency, the National Institute for Occupational Safety and Health, located in a different federal department (Health, Education, and Welfare, now Health and Human Services), that would do the research and provide the "criteria documents" on which OSHA would be required to base its standards. And as a final blow, the states (where business interests tend to be quite influential) were given the right to opt out and set up their own regulatory agencies, which roughly half the states then did. Who in their right mind, if they wanted OSHA to operate effectively, would have designed it this way? No one would. It was largely designed by its enemies, who wanted it to be weak, fragmented, and ineffective.[47]

Anyone who thinks a bureaucracy under congressional control can even remotely resemble a rational system of effective governance is just dreaming. The bureaucracy is a product of piecemeal decisions, it is intensely political, it is profoundly shaped by strategic jockeying among supporters and enemies—and it is an organizational mess that makes no intellectual sense. Like public policy, it is cobbled together bit by bit for political reasons that often have little to do with the rational application of expertise and organization.

The Larger System of Governance

Truth be told, though, the federal bureaucracy is the least of it. Most domestic policies adopted by Congress are administered through state and local governments, which members of Congress are eager to feed with programs and money. It is at those levels that most of the nation's public funds are spent and more than 80 percent of its public workers are employed. The US Department of Education, for example, is a huge conduit through which program-specific money flows to states and school districts around the country. The department is involved in monitoring, evaluating, setting standards, writing rules, and the like, but the programs are actually staffed and carried out by teachers and administrators at the local level who are not federal workers. Something similar happens for most other domestic programs, whether they deal with social welfare or the environment or transportation.[48]

And this massive delegation to state and local governments is just the beginning—for the federal government also implements its policies through a nebulous but quite enormous realm of seemingly nongovernmental activity that includes a vast array of business firms, public and private institutions, nonprofit organizations, and other actors that receive public money for acting on the government's behalf. The Defense Department does not make its own bombers or fighter airplanes but relies on aerospace companies like Lockheed Martin, which survive on billions of dollars of federal contracts. Social welfare programs of all sorts are carried out by diverse private organizations, including many that are religious, such as Catholic Charities USA. Lyndon Johnson's War on Poverty got traction on the ground through "community action agencies"—private groups in local communities—that propose and carry out local programs to help the needy. Medicare, Medicaid, and Obamacare all rely on private providers, such as doctors, hospitals, and pharmacies, to deliver medical services. Much the same is true of the nation's massive student loan programs, which are subsidized by the government but implemented by private banks, where students actually get (and later repay) their money.[49]

Conservatives may favor these sorts of governmental arrangements with firms, nonprofits, and other private actors because they seem to be market-based. But the fact is, for liberals and conservatives alike, these approaches also have purely political attractions. They allow legislators—including conservatives—to provide benefits to constituents without appearing to use government. And they can do it in ways that are often so complex and obscure that powerful groups can receive enormously valuable benefits without anyone else really knowing.

Put all these manifestations of the federal government together— the bureaucracy, state and local implementation, the vast network of contracting arrangements—and what do you have? A governmental system so ambiguous, so amorphous, so extensive, and so unbelievably complex that no one can understand it or even identify it. There is no agreed-upon name for this massive conglomeration of governmental pieces, but political scientist Steven Teles has offered one. He calls it a "kludgeocracy"—and he argues that, over the next decades, the national debate will not be about the size of government but about the kludgeocracy itself. As he puts it, "The issues that will define our major debates will concern the complexity of government, rather than its sheer scope. With that complexity has also come incoherence. . . . Understanding, describing, and addressing this problem of complexity and incoherence is the next great American political challenge."[50]

We agree. But we also think that the *ineffectiveness* of government goes hand in hand with its complexity and incoherence—and that the entire syndrome is rooted in Congress, and in the Constitution more generally. The kludgeocracy didn't emerge by accident. Members of Congress had incentives to build it, piece by piece. And build it they did.

A Way Out

Is there any way out of this mess? Congress can provide no solution, because it is the main culprit in this whole gory saga. For all sorts of reasons, the courts are no help either. With little incentive to create coherent or effective policy, and holding only meager substantive knowledge about the policy measures before them, federal judges cannot be expected to set things right. Indeed, much of the time they actually make things worse by using their formal authority to impose their own preferences on public policy—reaching in to change, weaken, omit, or reinterpret select provisions of any given policy, with potentially great damage to the policy's coherence and ultimate effectiveness.[51]

The president, however, is a very different breed of player. Unlike Congress—and unlike the courts—presidents are strongly driven to address important national problems by drawing upon the vast informational resources available to them, crafting coherent, effective policy solutions, getting them passed into law, and implementing them. The system being what it is, presidents are heavily constrained, and they have a very difficult time achieving their lofty goals. But despite it all, they are the champions of effective government—and if this nation is ever to escape its morass of a governance system, the presidency is the way out.

3

The Promise of Presidential Leadership

The nation is all too accustomed to the partisan and ideological divisions that often separate presidents and legislators. When they square off against one another as Democrats and Republicans, as liberals and conservatives, everyone expects to see sparks fly. And they do. Truth be told, though, the divisions between presidents and legislators run a good deal deeper than party and ideology—because the Constitution has seen to it that presidents and legislators are wired to be very different types of political actors. They see things differently. They care about different things. They evaluate policy on altogether different terms.

In view of Congress's built-in pathologies, anyone concerned about the capacity of American government to address the big, complex social problems of our times should see great promise in the fact that presidents are so fundamentally different—for they provide the nation with its best chance of rising above the parochialism and myopia in which legislators brew. They don't succeed nearly enough. Separation of powers ensures as much. But to the extent they are able, presidents use the authority, leverage, and resources at their disposal to elevate the national interest, to pursue long-term solutions to the nation's pressing problems, and to bring rationality and coherence to government as a whole—things that Congress simply cannot do.

In this chapter, we will explain why presidents are so different from legislators, and we'll show that this presidential difference—which shapes the behavior of *all* presidents, regardless of party—compels them, often against great political odds, to take on the special-interest forces within Congress in pushing for a more effective government. Such is the promise, all too rarely fulfilled, of presidential leadership.

A Brief Illustration: The Interstate Highway System

To Americans today, it seems basic, essential—and obvious—that our country should have an interstate highway system. And of course we do have such a system, a network of more than forty-two thousand miles of highway, devised during the late 1950s, that stitched a nation of backcountry roads and urban avenues into a coherent, interconnected whole, with massive consequences for urban development, trade, travel, and economic growth. The building of the interstate highway system was the largest public works program of the twentieth century, with an eventual price tag of some $125 billion—and it was well worth it. Without it, the nation would not be anywhere near as prosperous or connected as it is today.

Yet were it not for the vision of presidents, this crucial national need might not have been met. Congress lumbered toward addressing it—first in 1921, then again in 1938—by passing legislation intended to lend federal support to a national highway system.

But nothing of consequence came of these laws. Not until Franklin Roosevelt acted on his own authority to appoint an Interregional Highway Committee did serious plans get drafted for moving the nation ahead.[1] Even so, with Congress authorizing paltry sums of money, the initiative barely inched forward. By the mid-1950s, with Eisenhower now president, only 480 freeway miles had actually been built in the country's twenty-five largest cities.[2]

Eisenhower was not satisfied. Rather than engage Congress, he began by reaching out to his executive counterparts in state governments. Speaking through his vice president, he called upon the attendees of the annual state governors conference to lend their support to a new national highway system. "Our highway network is inadequate locally, and obsolete as a national system," Richard Nixon told them. The current system wasted billions of dollars due to detours and traffic jams, clogged the nation's courts with highway-related suits, delayed the transportation of goods, and resulted in "appalling inadequacies to meet the demands of catastrophe or defense, should an atomic war come." What was needed, Nixon argued, was a federal-state cooperative alliance to bring the new system.[3]

The speech had an "electrifying effect" on the conference, and, harnessing this energy, Eisenhower appointed a committee to draft specific plans for how the highway program might be funded. He then forwarded the committee's report to Congress in February 1955, appealing to long-term considerations about the national welfare: "Together, the united forces of our communication and transportation systems are dynamic elements in the very name we bear—United States. Without them, we would be a mere alliance of many separate parts."[4] If the nation was to flourish, the president insisted, it must develop a rational system of roads that would bind localities together into a common whole.

Left to their own devices, members of Congress could not possibly have devised an efficient system of highways traversing the nation—because only select districts and cities would be directly affected, and the rest would seem to "lose." But with the president providing the needed focus, plans, and legislative leadership, there was a way forward. Senator Albert Gore Sr. of Tennessee and Representative George H. Fallon of Baltimore introduced bills in their respective chambers to provide a basis for congressional action. Inevitably—Congress being what it is—these bills attracted considerable scrutiny from organized interests, and, after an intense lobbying campaign by trucking, petroleum, and tire interests, the first go-around ended in failure. Said Speaker Sam Rayburn, "The people who were going to have to pay for these roads put on a propaganda campaign that killed the bill."[5]

Eisenhower persevered. The next year his Bureau of Public Roads distributed to every member of Congress detailed plans showing how the proposed interstate highway system would benefit, directly or indirectly, each of their districts and states.[6] After key compromises were made on financing mechanisms, new bills were successfully navigated through both the House and Senate—and the president signed the Federal-Aid Highway Act into law on June 29, 1956.

This story is not the president's alone. Eisenhower did not get everything he wanted, and some members of Congress made important contributions. But if it hadn't been for Roosevelt's initial work in designing a plan and Eisenhower's energy and dedication in executing it, we most assuredly would not have witnessed such a massive, coordinated effort to build a rational network of interstate highways—a network that was absolutely crucial to the well-being of the nation. Congress was too fragmented, divided, and locally focused to make this project a reality. Presidential leadership was the key.

WHAT DISTINGUISHES PRESIDENTS FROM LEGISLATORS

As political actors, the presidents who envisioned a national highway system and orchestrated politics to make it a reality were quite different from the swarm of legislators who were mired in local concerns and special interests. This is no accident. Much the same could be said about the politics of most any important policy issue, regardless of the time period. Presidents are cut from a different cloth than legislators.

As we've seen, legislators are institutionally wired to view the world from a particular vantage point, one that is politically anchored to their districts and states. They are myopic in their approach to policy and narrowly concerned about the pieces of government rather than the whole. While we can clearly generalize about the commonalities of legislators—there are hundreds of them, after all, and we are essentially talking about central tendencies—one might look skeptically upon efforts to do the same for presidents. At any given time, there is just one president inhabiting the Oval Office. One FDR. One Eisenhower. One Obama. And it makes sense to think that idiosyncratic facts about each individual president—his personality, leadership style, past experience, ideology, disposition, and the like—drive the fundamentals of his presidency and provide the key to understanding why he does what he does.

But in most matters that really count, that just isn't so. While the personal characteristics of presidents surely do matter at the margins, the key to understanding presidential behavior lies in getting beyond the uniqueness of presidents as individuals and recognizing that, just as legislators are products of the American institutional system, so are presidents. All individuals who occupy the office of the president, whatever their personalities, whatever their backgrounds, are shaped in profoundly similar ways by their institutional location and the institutional forces acting upon them. They may well be very different people, but they are all presidents. And in the pulling and hauling of American politics, they think and act in ways that are distinctly presidential. Characteristic by characteristic, presidents stand in stark contrast to legislators.

Whereas members of Congress are parochial, presidents are national in outlook and orientation. While legislators are preoccupied with special interests and local constituencies, presidents set their sights on the nation as a whole and strive to represent the national interest, at least as they construe it. This happens not because presidents are public-spirited people with noble values. It happens because they have compelling, institutionally induced incentives to behave that way. Most obviously, they must appeal to national constituencies and put together national coalitions—of both elites and voters—in order to get their party's nomination and win the general election. Throughout the campaign, they need to present themselves as candidates with promising solutions to pressing national problems. And they do exactly that, rolling out policy agendas with titles like "Prosperity for America's Families" (Al Gore's in 2000), "Our Plan for America: Stronger at Home, Respected in the World" (Kerry and Edwards, 2004), "Change We Can Believe In: Barack Obama's Plan to Renew America's Promise" (Obama, 2008), or "Believe in America" (Romney, 2012)—hardly the stuff of parochial politicians. Presidential campaigns, like no others, are imbued with national emphasis and meaning.[7]

Once in office, their support coalition fully expects them to follow through on their campaign promises. But more than that, as single individuals endowed with executive authority, presidents inevitably become the focal point of American government, the recognized problem-solver in chief, and—although they lack the formal power to genuinely lead—they are expected to act forcefully and effectively on behalf of the nation as a whole. These expectations were weaker during the post–Civil War period, when presidents were beholden to party machines and Congress dominated politics. But as political scientist Stephen Skowronek observes, "The notion of a prior age when presidents did not *have* to be leaders—an age when vital national interests were only sporadically at the fore and most presidents could rest content with mere clerkship—is nothing more than a conceit of modern times."[8] That presidents were looked to as leaders of the nation, and expected to behave as such, has been a central feature of American politics from the beginning. It was strongly embedded in the political culture from Washington through Jefferson, Jackson, Polk, and Lincoln—and with the rise of Progressivism, Theodore Roosevelt, and the modern presidency, those expectations were ramped up further, demanding a much-heightened level of presidential activism, responsibility, and centrality.[9]

In carrying out that role, presidents do not have the constitutional authority to achieve what they want. But they do have a great practical advantage: precisely because their constituency is large in size and national in scope, it is filled with so many diverse and competing interests that presidents can rise above the fray and be far less responsive to special interest groups than members of

Congress need to be. Legislators are wired to be special-interest politicians and responsive to narrow parochial pressures. Presidents are not. Presidents are politicians, yes, and they want to win elections and amass enough political support to get their policy proposals through Congress. But their position of national leadership gives them far more freedom from special-interest pressure, and far more flexibility and opportunity to represent the national interest, than their legislative counterparts.

From their unique perch in American government, presidents see national problems like no one else. And these national problems are a good deal more than a weighted summation of the parochial problems facing each individual district and state in the country, which is all that Congress, left to its own devices, stands to represent. The problems that presidents discern touch upon issues of national fate, identity, welfare, and security. Though these problems may affect some portions of the country more strongly than others, they cannot be fully understood by reference to all their local manifestations. Solving them requires a shift in the very terms of debate. Fifty eyewitness accounts of what is best for each of the fifty states, and another 435 pleas for what is best for each of the 435 voting districts, do not add up to a coherent statement about what is best for the country as a whole. Only a presidential perspective can do that.

Whereas members of Congress are myopic, preoccupied by the short term, presidents are motivated by their legacies to focus on the long term. For every person who has occupied the office, the presidency has been the apex of his career—and, most likely, of his entire life. Although more than a few former presidents have sought to return to the White House, only John Quincy Adams and Andrew Johnson later served in Congress, while William Howard Taft went on to the Supreme Court. All others spent their post-presidency years permanently retired from elective office, engaged in activities aimed at bolstering the case that they were outstanding national leaders and that their tenures in office made a big positive difference. The fact is, all presidents have recognized that, in the grander scheme of their lives, the presidency was it for them—their once-in-a-lifetime opportunity to fulfill their highest ambitions and make their mark on the world. And so, once elected the nation's leader, their attentions turn to their place in history.[10]

Presidents care profoundly about how future generations will evaluate them, particularly future generations of opinion leaders: historians, social scientists, and other close observers of American politics who are in a position to judge a president's accomplishments and compare them to those of other presidents. And how do presidents get judged in the eyes of history? By their policy achievements, and by the extent to which those achievements—like the Louisiana Purchase or the New Deal or Medicare—addressed major national problems in ways that proved durable and far-reaching. It is no coincidence that Franklin Delano Roosevelt is routinely the most highly ranked president of modern times, because his policy achievements were massive and monumental, transforming the structure of American government—with many of his policies still in place to this day. It is also no coincidence that Bill Clinton is not so highly ranked. For even though he was (and still is) popular with the American people, with Republicans in control of Congress his policy achievements were modest.

All presidents know that significant policy achievements are the coin of the realm and that, to go down in history as strong, successful leaders, they must take on truly national problems, push for coherent solutions, and think about how these policies and their consequences will play out over the long term. Their success will be judged not simply by what they accomplish while in office but also by what those accomplishments mean and entail for the future of the nation and its citizens' well-being. At their motivational core, then, presidents are strikingly different from legislators and approach public policy in a completely different way. They must, of course, play the legislative game to get anything done—so presidents cannot avoid catering to the parochialism of legislators, giving in to some of their cobbled-together concoctions, engaging in pork-barrel politics, and otherwise departing from the policy paths they would prefer to follow. But the premium they place on legacy makes them champions of the nation's long-term interests in ways that Congress cannot and never will be.

Whereas members of Congress concern themselves with the pieces, presidents think about the whole. If policy is to be effective, it must be coherently designed as a well-integrated, intellectually justifiable whole. If government is to be effective, it must be endowed with a coherent organizational structure that is suited to high performance. As we have seen, Congress is not merely incapable of designing policy and government to meet these standards, it actually has no intention of doing so, because its members are motivated to think and act in terms of the parts rather than the whole. This is not true of presidents. Presidents are driven to think in national terms about problems and solutions, they are obsessed with gaining legacies as strong, successful leaders—and they are propelled, as a result, to approach policy and government in holistic terms. They seek policies that are coherent, well integrated, and effective. And they seek a government that is coherent, well integrated, and effective.[11]

Presidents cannot have what they seek—at least not with any regularity. They operate in a constitutional system that underpowers them, ensuring that they will be only partially successful at best and forcing them to adapt to other power holders—legislators and interest groups—in order to get even a portion of what they want. They need to be political and strategic; they need to compromise at every turn; and they usually cannot prevent their best-laid policy designs from being corrupted, weakened, and dismembered if anything at all is to pass. Throughout the policy process, however, presidents stand out as the nation's key force for good government. For them, cobbled-together policies are not desirable, and they fight hard to avoid precisely the kinds of legislative conglomerations that Congress is so happy to produce. Unlike most members of Congress, presidents have strong incentives to push hard for policies that *are* coherent and *do* work—because these are the policies for which they will be remembered and on which their legacies are determined. Presidents are the champions of coherence and effectiveness in a fragmented, parochial political world.

This same logic extends to the structure of government. The president is the chief executive, and his control over the executive branch—the bureaucracy—is perhaps the key means by which he exercises power over American public policy. He is hardly unimpeded. Separation of powers sees to that. Congress actively uses its control over budgets, programs, oversight, and much more to try to influence executive agencies, and the courts use their judicial powers to prevent, redirect, and shape agency behaviors as well—with the net result that agencies are pulled in many directions, policies are rendered incoherent, authority is fragmented, and the bureaucracy is in disarray. This is the reality—but presidents have strong incentives to fight against these organizational perversities.

What presidents want is a rational, well-designed structure of government that has the capacity for effective performance and that, as chief executives, they can lead from above. Over the years, they have relentlessly deployed institutional mechanisms—among them the Bureau of the Budget (now the Office of Management and Budget), the Council of Economic Advisers, the National Security Council, policy committees within the White House, the Office of Information and Regulatory Affairs (within OMB), and White House legislative liaison operations—that allow them to exercise greater, more rational, more centralized control over the entire structure of government. And they have made extensive use of their appointment powers and their powers of unilateral action to move policy and government in directions consistent with their policy agendas.

Presidents remain underpowered. But they have succeeded in shifting the *balance* of power in their favor, particularly since the Progressive transition to modern government and the rising demands for presidential action that have accompanied it. They have used every ounce of that power to try to establish their legacies as great leaders. Presidents are not really in charge. No one is. But in the fractious world of American politics, they are the champions of coherent, effective government—and they are the only major actors who are truly thinking about the whole, not just the parts.

THERE ARE NO LEGISLATORS ON MOUNT RUSHMORE

We are not saying here that presidents are secular gods of some sort. They are not perfect. Their policy agendas may be informed by patently partisan considerations. And sometimes they make decisions that turn out to be very bad for the country—such as, many would argue, when George W. Bush took the nation to war in Iraq. But in a separation-of-powers system that is deeply rooted in parochialism and fragmentation and that makes effective government virtually impossible, presidents hold extraordinary promise. *They are special.* They are wired to pursue the national interest, to fight against parochialism, to seek coherent solutions to the nation's problems, to seek a rational, well-working bureaucracy—and to build and use power toward those ends.

If there is one motivator that most forcefully drives presidential behavior, it is their concerns about legacy. That presidents care about their legacies is much talked about, and even joked about, in popular discussions of the presidency. But rarely is it taken seriously as the key driver of what presidents do. That being so, we want to devote some additional attention to it here in order to shine a brighter light on its importance.

Whatever their parties, whatever their personalities, presidents have a burning desire to be remembered as great leaders. They want subsequent generations of citizens to look back on their time in office and pay homage to their accomplishments—and this shapes the policies they pursue and the problems they take on. Consider Lyndon Johnson, for example. He wasn't just a liberal president with a liberal policy agenda. He was a man who was determined to use the office of the presidency to do great things for America—and to make *himself* great in the eyes of the nation. He put it well, and explicitly, in his 1965 address to Congress asking for their support of the Voting Rights Act:

> I want to be the president who educated young children to the wonders of their world. I want to be the president who helped to feed the hungry and to prepare them to be taxpayers instead

of tax-eaters. I want to be the president who helped the poor to find their own way and who protected the right of every citizen to vote in every election. I want to be the president who helped to end hatred among his fellow men and who promoted love among the people of all races and all regions and all parties. I want to be the president who helped to end war among the brothers of this earth.[12]

Lyndon Johnson was hardly unique. All presidents harbor these same sorts of aspirations. They want to leave their distinctive mark on the world. They want to be regarded as great. They want to make the most of their golden opportunity. It doesn't always turn out that way, of course, as presidents face a complex, contentious world and a plethora of uncertain choices. They are not in control of their own fates—or their own legacies. But they do try. Incessantly and single-mindedly.

As for Lyndon Johnson, he would go on to enact all sorts of legislation expressly intended to realize his lofty objectives. The Vietnam War, though, would derail his presidency, along with his plans for seeking a second elected term. After stepping down in 1969, he worried constantly that he would be remembered as the architect of the Vietnam War and not as the force behind the most significant body of domestic legislation since the New Deal. And he was right to worry, because Vietnam has been a blight on his legacy ever since and prevented him from being regarded as one of the truly great leaders this nation has ever had—a legacy that might otherwise have been his.[13]

And then there is Richard Nixon, whose otherwise productive presidency, and with it his legacy, was undone by the Watergate scandal (and also Vietnam). Ironically, the crucial evidence that linked the hotel burglary to the president was found in a White House taping system that Nixon himself had approved with an eye toward history's judgment. When Alexander Butterfield, Nixon's deputy assistant, revealed the existence of the tapes to the Senate Select Committee on Presidential Campaign Activities, which was investigating the unfolding Watergate scandal, he remarked, "The President is very history-oriented and history-conscious about the role he is going to play."[14] In this way, Nixon was hardly exceptional. Lyndon Johnson himself had installed a taping system for much the same reason. But Nixon would ultimately make history not for his accomplishments, as he had anticipated, but for the scandal that the tapes revealed. In forced retirement, Nixon would later work doggedly to try to ensure that his legacy amounted to something more than Watergate. He advised presidents. He wrote numerous books on US foreign policy. He traveled the globe. And he did all this as part of a deliberate effort to refashion his identity and secure an exalted place in the nation's history—which had been his goal all along.

George W. Bush's presidency provides another case in point. Bush sought to establish his legacy with big policy achievements: No Child Left Behind, a huge tax cut, the addition of prescription-drug coverage to Medicare, and—not least—the launching of major wars in Afghanistan and Iraq. By the time he left office, though, the economy was in free fall, NCLB was proving contentious, the tax cuts had greatly exacerbated the nation's deficit problems, Republicans were blaming him for vast overspending (in part due to the Medicare reform), and both wars were proving expensive, unwinnable, and unpopular. Bush's approval ratings were in the low thirties. Still, he held on to the persistent hope that history would vindicate the decisions he had made while in office.

He repeatedly compared himself to Harry Truman, who was exco-
riated while in the White House but subsequently reaped praise
from historians and the public. And in his memoirs, Bush insisted
that he had been unaffected by the storm of negativity surrounding
his tenure in office. For him, the endless debates about a president's
legacy offered reason for optimism. As he put it, "If they're still assessing George Washington's legacy two centuries after he left office,
this George W. doesn't have to worry about today's headlines."[15]

It is not just presidents who are thinking about their legacies.
So too do the audiences that matter most to them. Historians scour
the records of each president, attempting to discern his unique
contribution. They evaluate presidents not on ephemera—on their
popularity or their political skills or their responsiveness to local
populations—but rather on accomplishments that reach broadly,
that endure long after their time in office, and that meaningfully
address important problems. Likewise, journalists and media pun-
dits cast about looking for clues to how each sitting president will
be viewed by history. Various organizations, such as the Miller
Center at the University of Virginia and PBS in its "The Presidents"
film series, systematically gauge the legacy of each individual president. And for the last half century, pollsters also have evaluated
the "greatness" of each president—with the likes of Washington,
Lincoln, and FDR routinely at the top of the rankings, and Hard-
ing, Buchanan, and Andrew Johnson anchoring the bottom. The
first such poll was conducted by the historian Arthur Schlesinger
Sr., who in 1948 saw a need to sort out what makes a president
great—or a failure. Subsequently, Schlesinger's son—Arthur
Schlesinger Jr., who himself would go on to write some of the most
influential books on the American presidency of the late twentieth
century—picked up the charge and conducted similar polls in

1962 and 1996. Following suit, many more pollsters have solicited the opinions of political scientists, historians, and journalists about how each president ranks against the others.[16]

Presidents, then, have every incentive to do great things by enacting major policies that beneficially affect the country as a whole for generations to come. This drive to greatness is built into the presidential office and shared by everyone who occupies it. If earmarks and pork-barrel projects are what legislators yearn for, presidents deal in grand plans and systemic reforms. They must often settle for much less, of course. But what presidents want is to realize historic ambitions—to remake health care, to modernize the government, to reorient the nation's standing on the international stage, to solve the vexing problems of debt or poverty or a warming climate. Presidents take actions that are meant to reverberate through the ages.

And they do not stop when their terms in office come to an end. Onward they push, trying to extend their records of accomplishments long after they have left the White House. And those presidents who faltered in office—think Hoover, Nixon, or Carter—worked with particular zeal as ex-presidents to build a legacy worthy of praise from the future historians who would judge them.

Presidential libraries are nothing if not monuments to legacy. And without exception, presidents themselves are deeply involved in their creation and operation. FDR was the first president to build a library, which was constructed in a Hyde Park, New York, Dutch colonial that, in his view, symbolized "a quality of endurance against great odds—a quality of quiet determination to conquer obstacles of nature and obstacles of man."[17] Since then, every president has constructed a library of his own with the express purpose of not only housing historical artifacts but also informing the writing of history. Through the archival materials they organize, the presentations they build, and the accomplishments they herald, presidential libraries make the best case possible for a president's rightful place in history. In some instances, as with Lyndon Johnson, libraries attempt to redefine the terms of greatness by emphasizing achievements (his incredible production of domestic legislation during the 79th Congress) and downplaying failures (the disaster that was Vietnam). In others—for example, with Nixon—libraries offer a salve to scandal. And in others still, as for Reagan, libraries make the case in the most forceful terms possible that certain presidents altered the trajectory of world events. But for all, presidential libraries function as persistent and lasting tributes to a president's legacy.

While presidents serve in office, all sorts of events disrupt the gaze that they keep on the distant horizon. An upcoming election, a scandal within their ranks, or a sudden drop in the polls can shake presidents from their reverie. But most everything they scramble to deal with in the moment is done with an eye to the legacy that is ultimately being built—and to the historians who will judge them. Presidents do not merely hold out hope that historians will remember them. Presidents seek to change history itself.

PRESIDENTIAL DIFFERENCE, CONGRESSIONAL REACTION

We can see strong, clear evidence of the president's distinctive characteristics and motivations in all sorts of contemporary debates. Here we provide just a few illustrations, chosen because they allow us to take a look at the politics surrounding some of the most pressing problems facing the nation in modern times: health care, energy independence, social security, and climate change.

The point of these studies is not to blindly salute the president, to exalt every presidential policy as infinitely wise or the one best way. The point, rather, is to illuminate the distinct ways in which presidents see, understand, and approach the nation's major problems and potential solutions to them—and to contrast what presidents do with what Congress does. In every case, the pattern is the same. Regardless of party, regardless of ideology, presidents push hard to craft and enact effective solutions to the nation's vexing problems, but they run into a minefield of special-interest pressures and resistance in Congress.

The Long Presidential Struggle for Health-Care Reform

America's health-care system is wholly unique among modernized nations: it is hugely expensive, vastly unequal in its coverage, and incredibly inefficient. In 2012, the average health care cost for US citizens was $8,508, while in Britain the average cost was $3,405. Yet all this money does not buy better health care: compared to other developed democracies, the United States ranks last in terms of efficiency, equity, and outcomes. Even with the adoption of the Affordable Care Act, over thirty million Americans are still without coverage, and many of those covered do not have insurance packages sufficient to meet their needs. As a result, many Americans—especially poor Americans—avoid preventive care, leading to medical ailments that ultimately cost society far more than preventive treatments would have. These same uninsured, moreover, often go to emergency rooms, where taxpayers end up footing the whole bill in one way or another. In short, America pays an exorbitant price for a health-care system that simply doesn't do the job for society as a whole.[18]

For more than eighty years, presidents have consistently recognized the social importance of the problem—and Democrats and Republicans alike have sought to do something about it. They have made proposals. They have taken action. But until Barack Obama achieved his legislative breakthrough with the Affordable Care Act in 2010—which was only a partial victory for reform, as we've already seen—their reformist efforts were met with strident opposition from Congress. The result, most often, was that Congress did nothing. And when it did act, it disgorged patchwork policies that did not add up to a coherent, well-working system. The nation has a bizarre health-care system because that is what Congress has given it—despite the best efforts of presidents.

The history of presidents trying to shape health-care policy goes all the way back to Theodore Roosevelt. TR's cousin Franklin Roosevelt, though, was the first to make a serious move in this policy domain. FDR came to office in 1933 and benefited from huge Democratic majorities in both chambers of Congress. He sought to include health care as a part of his new proposal for the Social Security program—a lynchpin of his New Deal—but the southern Democratic chairmen who ruled the relevant committees were not willing to budge on the issue. In addition, the lobbying power of doctors via the American Medical Association (AMA) was considerable; and the AMA, along with allies in the hospital and insurance industries, was prepared to pounce on any legislation that changed the status quo. Roosevelt and his advisers were sure that including health insurance in the final version of the Social Security Act would result in the defeat of the entire bill, so they reluctantly set health care aside. The special interests won.[19]

The presidential fight for comprehensive health-care reform, however, was carried on by Roosevelt's successor, Harry Truman.

In November of 1945, Truman delivered a speech to Congress exhorting it to create a national health insurance fund run by the federal government. "Millions of our citizens," he argued, "do not now have a full measure of opportunity to achieve and enjoy good health. Millions do not now have protection or security against the economic effects of sickness. The time has arrived for action to help them attain that opportunity and that protection."[20] The optional fund would be open to all Americans, who would pay monthly fees into the insurance pool. The government would set payment structures for doctors, and doctors could decide whether they wanted to participate in the program. Predictably, however, Truman faced much the same opposition that Roosevelt had in Congress—only worse, for now the Republicans had a much larger contingent. His first proposal never saw the light of day.

Still, Truman did not abandon the effort. Indeed, he made health care a central plank of his 1948 election campaign. Not only did Truman win the election but Democrats gained seventy-five seats in Congress, earning the party a clear majority and a wide mandate for health-care reform. The AMA, however, pulled out its political knives. Echoing popular concerns about the dangers of socialism, the AMA ran a public relations campaign labeling the president's plan as "socialized medicine"—and in alliance with conservative committee chairs, made sure that the bill never made it to the floor for a vote.

As we discussed in the last chapter, a system of employer-based insurance began to evolve during World War II as industries sought to avoid wage-price controls by using health insurance benefits to attract talented labor. As this system spread, many workers gained. But such insurance only extended to individuals fortunate enough to be employed (and by companies that actually offered it). Many millions of Americans were not so fortunate, particularly the poor, the unemployed, the self-employed, and the elderly. There were huge and inevitable holes in the system. Indeed, it wasn't really a system. It was just a private set of benefits that emerged on its own, with tax help from the government—and it *was never designed or intended to be a coherent system.*

John F. Kennedy, who assumed the presidency in 1961, aspired to change this. In light of the failed efforts under Truman, many reformers had come to believe during the 1950s that they could only overcome the usual congressional obstacles—including, notably, the blocking power of southern committee chairs—by paring back their goals. A lot. And Kennedy and his advisers saw the strategic wisdom in that. It wasn't desirable, but it was necessary. They decided not to pursue health-care coverage for all Americans but rather to focus just on the elderly—who were not only a vulnerable and needy subgroup of the population but also a high-risk group that was less attractive to insurance companies. Yet even this reduction in scope didn't work. Despite high public support, Kennedy's Medicare bill for the elderly went down in flames. He immediately went on television to declare this the "most serious defeat for every American family."[21]

Kennedy's assassination in late 1963, however, gave way to Lyndon Johnson's landslide victory in 1964, accompanied by massive Democratic majorities—liberal majorities—in both chambers. For the next two years, the nation underwent a rare political experience that rivaled the first few years of the New Deal: the political doors were swung open wide for major reform. Medicare, moreover, enjoyed top billing. It had been a salient issue on which Johnson and congressional Democrats had campaigned, and it became the exclusive focus of Johnson's 1965 State of the Union speech setting out the president's agenda. Southern Democrats still controlled key committees, but they now had strong reason to be more conciliatory, knowing that Johnson and the liberals had overwhelming numbers. Even so, the powerful AMA remained stridently opposed to Medicare, worrying about federal control of doctors and their fees. And other powerful industry groups, representing insurance companies and hospitals, among others, remained vigilant in protecting their interests and shaping the contours of the bill.[22]

The outcome was a win for the president: a major political achievement, given all the failures of the past. The nation got Medicare—and as part of the same bill, it also got Medicaid, a state-administered insurance program for the poor. Yet the bill was passed "in the most 'American' of fashions: in the final analysis, everyone was bought off and no faction had its interests directly assaulted."[23] We won't go into the details, but here is the big picture. Medicare was designed to drastically limit the federal government's involvement in key decisions—for example, in controlling costs (which soon skyrocketed). It also accommodated the interests, and put decision-making in the hands, of the key operators that were deeply entrenched in running the existing system: insurance companies, hospitals, doctors, and others. The resulting healthcare "system" that it gave the nation was also typical, consisting of employer-based insurance for (most) people with jobs, Medicare for the elderly, Medicaid for the poor—and nothing for millions of others. It was not really a system at all but rather a patchwork with big holes—and as time would show, a very, very expensive patchwork indeed that remained woefully inadequate as an effective solution to the nation's serious health-care problems.

By the early 1970s, health-care costs were already on the rise, and steeply. Recognizing as much, Republican president Richard

Nixon proposed a reform in 1971 to expand coverage and make the system more cost-effective—and it went nowhere in Congress. Still, he didn't give up. Nixon returned with a much more far-reaching proposal for universal health care, his Comprehensive Health Insurance Act—telling Congress in February 1974, "Comprehensive health insurance is an idea whose time has come."[24] A great many others thought so too, and Congress was awash in competing health-care proposals; indeed, the Senate Finance Committee "had to consider seven serious health care proposals emanating from every possible health care interest."[25] And with so many competing interests and powerful players involved, Congress ground to a halt. Nixon's pursuit of universal health care failed. So did a follow-up effort by Gerald Ford after Nixon's resignation.

Jimmy Carter came into office in 1977 with big Democratic majorities—a rebuke to Republicans following the Watergate scandal—and comprehensive health-care reform was high on his agenda. Leaders of both parties felt, as Nixon had, that the time was right for it to finally pass. Yet with all the newly elected members of Congress pushing for greater influence within their institution, the committee system became more decentralized—spreading the power around, and with it the potential for blocking. More committees would now be involved in any given health bill, and the difficulties of navigating the legislative process would be magnified. Carter decided, as a result, to first propose a more limited health-care reform that just dealt with the problem of rising costs—and once that passed, to present his major proposal for universal health care. You can guess where this is going. The proposal to control medical costs was stridently opposed by "every major medical lobby," including the AMA and the American Hospital Association—and it went down to defeat (multiple times).[26]

Needless to say, Carter's plan for universal health care never went anywhere either.

Health-care costs continued to rise throughout the 1980s, as did the percentage of individuals without insurance—and Bill Clinton, having campaigned hard on the issue during his 1992 presidential campaign, quickly made universal health care the centerpiece of his policy agenda. Once again, the time seemed to be right. And he was advantaged—as Johnson and Carter had been—with Democratic majorities in both houses. His strategy, though, was markedly different from that of the other presidents: he put his wife, Hillary Rodham Clinton, in charge of a vast task force of some five hundred advisers, experts, and industry representatives—circumventing Congress in an ongoing process of policy formulation run by the White House. Only after the ideas were fully developed and crafted, in a proposal running a thousand pages in length, were they submitted to Congress. The proposed system involved "managed care competition" within "regional alliances" and imposed an insurance mandate on employers. We won't describe it here. What matters is that, although powerful medical industry and business interests were on board in the beginning, they soon defected and went on the warpath—and once the proposal was introduced to Congress, it died fast and hard. Congressional Democrats offered compromise proposals, but those failed as well. The result was one of the greatest policy fiascos in modern American history.[27]

The pattern throughout the post-war era is as clear as it can be: recognizing that the nation has a profound and persistent health-care problem, particularly with respect to coverage and cost, presidents of both parties have regularly taken the lead in trying to do something about it—crafting coherent policy proposals that, in their judgment, offer effective solutions in the national interest. The policies themselves may or may not have been the best possible solutions. That is something experts can debate. But presidents regularly took on the challenge and sought to solve this vexing problem on behalf of the nation. And the result? Well-positioned members of Congress and powerful special interests combined to ensure that all these presidential efforts went nowhere. And what did Congress do to solve this problem itself? Nothing of any consequence.

What, then, about Barack Obama's Affordable Care Act (ACA) of 2010—which actually "succeeded"? The ACA is the most extensive set of American health-care reforms in decades, making it an extraordinary legislative feat, and it rightly stands as Obama's signature domestic policy achievement during his two terms in office. Yet its passage by Congress was possible precisely because it falls far short of the type of comprehensive reform that advocates had long sought. It falls short because, with the Clinton disaster very much in mind, Obama allowed Congress to patch together a bill its members could agree upon, with powerful interest groups doing much of the stitching.

From a political distance, one might think that the Democrats controlling Congress were driven by ideology to make good on the liberal dream of universal health care. And there may be some truth to that. But look *inside* the bill and what do we see? What is its actual content? The Affordable Care Act is riddled with appeasements, perks, and compromises that reflect the needs and desires of insurance companies, the AMA, hospitals, pharmaceutical companies, trial attorneys, employers that provide private insurance, and other special-interest groups. In its policy details, the ACA is best understood not as a liberal creation but simply as a *legislative* creation—and thus a creation heavily shaped by powerful special interests.

As we discussed in Chapter 2, the innovation in health insurance that emerged from the ACA was a major change from the past, but it was not really a new system. It was another cobbled-together congressional concoction, grafted onto the existing base of employer-provided health insurance—giving the nation a reformed system that no one would have designed that way had they started from the ground up and that did little to drastically reduce the nation's staggering cost burden.[28]

The Presidential Quest for Energy Independence

Sometimes, solutions to societal problems come not from a political breakthrough but from the advent and widespread adoption of a new technology. There is no more striking example than the expanding use of hydraulic fracturing, or "fracking," a technology that uses high-pressured water mixtures to tap gas reserves trapped in underground rock formations that were impervious to older extraction methods.

Recent fracking methods have yielded a dramatic increase in oil and gas development, particularly in shale reservoir rocks previously considered too impermeable for exploration. Between 2000 and 2010, fracking was utilized in the Appalachian Mountains, Gulf Coast, and Permian Basin. The result has been a massive increase in domestic oil and gas production. According to the most recent government forecast, in 2016 the United States will import only 23 percent of the crude oil it uses, the lowest level since 1970. The United States currently produces 9.4 million barrels per day (bpd), with 4.6 million barrels (49 percent) generated from fracking. Within the next five years, the United States is slated to produce 11.6 million barrels a day. During the same period, the output of Saudi Arabia is expected to drop from 11.7 million bpd to 10.6 million bpd.[29]

There is an ongoing debate about fracking's environmental repercussions. Environmental groups have expressed serious concerns about the high usage of water resources, the production of large quantities of wastewater, the injection of chemicals underground, and the potential impact on water resources above ground. Eerily, places like the state of Oklahoma are now experiencing hundreds of new earthquakes that seismologists attribute to hydraulic fracturing. Even so, a number of government reports have presented evidence and analysis that fail to confirm the environmentalists' worst fears and that tend to bolster confidence in the method's environmental safety. The EPA's Office of Research and Development argues that hydraulic fracturing, if done correctly, has no discernible impact on local water supplies.[30]

Debates about the environmental impacts of hydraulic fracturing will surely continue. For the time being, though, the advent of fracking has all but settled another issue that vexed energy-minded policymakers for decades. By massively increasing the supply of domestic gas production, fracking has substantially reduced the nation's dependence on foreign energy supplies. This is a very big deal. For decades, our political system tried and failed to produce a comprehensive energy policy, hoping to disentangle the United States from autocratic governments in oil-producing regions of South America and the Middle East. The recent wars in Iraq lent newfound urgency to the problem—but efforts to solve it go back decades, to the 1970s, when pursuit of a comprehensive energy policy was at the top of the nation's policy agenda.

It is worth recalling this earlier era, for it reveals a pattern similar to more contemporary efforts at government problem-solving. The plotline is familiar, with presidents leading the charge on matters of pressing national importance and members of Congress blocking them. First Nixon, then Ford and, most aggressively, Carter attempted to direct the nation toward an effective policy to promote energy independence. And each failed, in no small part because they confronted a Congress that engaged the issue on much more parochial terms.

Presidents had the facts on their side. The crisis of 1973, prompted by the Yom Kippur War and the subsequent OPEC embargo, caused the price of an oil barrel to quadruple and left consumers paying about 40 percent more at the pump than they had paid only several months before. With supply shortfalls came rationing, which in turn led to long lines of angry drivers waiting to fill up their tanks. That the OPEC nations were profiting off of the crisis fed an acute sense of anxiety about America's global standing. More to the point, critics worried that America's dependence on oil distorted the nation's foreign policy. Rather than keeping a wide berth around the autocratic regimes of the Middle East, the United States was becoming increasingly entangled in them. And the result, played out again and again, was an accommodation of repressive governments—and an ongoing danger of direct involvement and even war—that violated both the interests and democratic identities of the American nation.[31]

Policy was in shambles. Federal regulations dating back to the 1950s capped the amount of foreign oil that could be imported. The quotas, however, were designed for a different time, when demand was much lower. When President Eisenhower announced them, the United States was importing 965,000 barrels of crude oil a month. By 1973, when Nixon removed the caps, that number had swelled to 3.2 million.[32] Even with domestic oil production operating at peak levels, supply simply could not keep up with demand. With the problem situated at the intersection of federal regulations and international affairs, a national solution was in order.

Enter calls for energy independence. Weaning America off of foreign oil would not only benefit consumers who otherwise faced rising prices and rationed supplies, it would once again make the country master of its own affairs abroad. To become energy independent, Americans would need to conserve more and spend more; but in the long run, many believed, the benefits to international security and economic stability would justify the costs. Three successive presidents tried to make it happen.

At the height of the 1973 energy crisis, Richard Nixon announced Project Independence, which inaugurated the executive branch's drive toward energy independence. "In the spirit of Apollo, with the determination of the Manhattan Project," Nixon pledged that America would be extricated from foreign oil by 1980. Of course, such ambitions were no match for Watergate, which soon sank his presidency. But President Ford picked up where Nixon had left off. Ford proposed building 200 nuclear power plants and 250 new coal mines and developing other new domestic supply sources. In line with Nixon's proposals, Ford sought to end quotas and replace them with tariffs, thereby spurring industry to generate additional domestic sources. "The American people and many of our friends abroad have been waiting to see whether the executive and legislative branches of our government could reach agreement on the basic framework of a national energy policy," said Ford upon announcing the legislation.[33]

They would be left waiting. Ford's proposals were attacked by politicians from oil-consuming states, who claimed their constituents could not tolerate higher prices. House Speaker Tip O'Neill described energy as perhaps the "most parochial issue" that had ever come before Congress.[34] Lowering prices meant pleasing the consuming states, mostly located in the Northeast, but frustrating the producing states, largely in the South and Southwest. Conversely, increasing prices would only anger the consuming states and please the producing ones. The result was a Gordian knot the legislative branch could not untangle. And so late in his term, Ford was left to settle for a law, the Energy Policy and Conservation Act, that offered modest advances on conservation but did nothing to solve the core challenge of energy independence.

Into the breach stepped Jimmy Carter. His commitment to energy reform ran deeper than that of his predecessors. "We desperately needed a comprehensive program," the president wrote in his memoirs. As he told the nation at the time, responding to the energy crisis would require nothing less than "the moral equivalent of war."[35]

Shortly after taking office, Carter announced a comprehensive energy plan that was explicitly designed to promote the national interest, even if it took a toll on short-term popular support. These "unpopular" proposals, Carter said, would cause "inconveniences" and "sacrifices"—but would do the hard work of transitioning to a new world of rising demand and ever-diminishing supply. This would be accomplished by relying more heavily on domestic sources and by implementing an "equalization tax," which would raise domestic prices and then send the accumulated additional revenues back to consumers. If implemented, Carter's plan would increase stateside coal production by two-thirds, fit at least 2.5 million households for solar panels, and insulate 90 percent of all homes. Together, Carter explained, these initiatives would expedite America's march to an era of "peace, independence and freedom."[36]

The proposal's chances for passage appeared bright at first. Speaker O'Neill rushed it through the House with only minimal changes. Upon reaching the Senate, however, the bill confronted the same parochial forces that had doomed Ford's initiatives. The senators from consuming states had no interest in promoting price increases, and the senators from oil-producing states had no interest in promoting conservation. The pressure from lobbyists was also fierce. "The influence of the special interest lobbies is almost unbelievable, particularly from the automobile and oil industries," Carter wrote in his diary in June 1977.[37]

In 1978, a weakened bill finally passed. It had been shorn of the equalization tax that had been its centerpiece, and in the words of *Congressional Quarterly*, "promised to have little effect on the way Americans produced and consumed increasing quantities of energy." Instead, the legislation established new efficiency standards and tax credits for select industries. And like Ford's before him, Carter's effort to raise prices had the opposite effect, as the enacted bill actually cut taxes on cars that did not meet certain fuel standards (the so-called gas guzzlers tax). Given the irreconcilable interests of oil-producing and oil-consuming states, getting a tax increase through Congress proved impossible.[38]

By 1979 the energy crisis was magnified against the backdrop of an imploding Iran (a major oil producer). Carter tried to boost his prospects for reform by deploying the bully pulpit—giving, with great fanfare, what later came to be known (ignominiously) as his "malaise speech." In it, he played the role of southern preacher, exhorting Americans to "use car pools or public transportation," to pay attention to their thermostats, and to "avoid unnecessary trips." As a guiding objective, "conservation" came to replace "energy independence." The new ambition was to reduce dependence from its peak rather than achieve independence in its entirety. Taking a page from Nelson Rockefeller, Carter proposed the creation of a government-backed Energy Security Corporation, which would be charged with subsidizing commercial synthetic fuels, and an Energy Mobilization Board, which would accelerate the process by which energy proposals would be reviewed.[39]

The same story played out. At first, the speech was met with warm responses. Carter's approval ratings increased, and leaders from both sides of the aisle applauded his effort, as did the heads of the AFL-CIO and DuPont. Indeed, the Senate majority leader and the Speaker of the House anticipated passage within six months. But once again, the proposals were bottled up in Congress, whose members stripped the bills of their boldest ideas. The law that passed a year later contained the Energy Security Corporation but jettisoned the Energy Mobilization Board (and all the regulatory expedience it stood to offer). Ultimately, the new law did make modest improvements in conservation. Yet given America's continued reliance on foreign oil for at least three more decades, the law obviously did not deliver energy independence.[40]

For all his policy blueprints and personal passion, Carter's efforts to achieve energy independence met the same fates as Nixon's and Ford's. For this outcome, Carter perhaps deserves a share of the blame. He could have done more to shore up support in his own party. His relationship, or lack thereof, with Senator Russell Long, leader of the legislators from oil-producing states, appears comical in retrospect. "I never know what [Russell] is going to do—except screw me most of the time," Carter confided to one of his cabinet members.[41] And the president's hectoring tone did not play well with a public exhausted by crises and price hikes.

Yet none of the opposition offered an equally comprehensive alternative. They denied neither the problem nor its scope; they only pronounced the president's plans unacceptable. In so doing, federal lawmakers guarded their local turf jealously, never sacrificing for the national interest. They spent considerable resources investigating the oil companies on suspicions of price gouging—a worthy task, perhaps, but no substitute for proposing a solution of genuinely national proportions.[42] As a result, by the end of the decade, three successive presidents had tried and failed to confront a national problem that no one could deny—but no one, aside from presidents, was willing to tackle and solve.

Decades would pass before major change would occur and the nation would actually approach its goal of energy independence. Because the jury is still out on whether fracking is compatible with a healthy environment, it remains unclear how successful this change will prove to be in the grander scheme of things. But in terms of energy independence alone, it has been a spectacular success—a success that is almost entirely due to the driving force of the private marketplace and technological innovation, and not to effective policies on the part of the government. Presidents tried. But Congress stood in the way, immobilized, awash in special interests—and totally incapable of doing what it took to get the nation off foreign oil.

George W. Bush Grapples with Social Security Reform

As a program, Social Security has been wildly popular and had clear, positive impacts. In the first fifty years of its operation, this insurance program reduced the poverty rate of senior citizens from over 33 percent to less than 10 percent. But with baby boomers looking to retire, the average age of citizens steadily increasing, and payouts on the rise, the program faces new fiscal challenges—and this has been apparent for some time. According to a 2004 Bush-era report by the nonpartisan Congressional Budget Office (CBO), by 2019 Social Security would begin giving out more than it takes in, and by 2052 the "trust fund" it uses to finance benefits would be completely depleted. Uncorrected, the CBO concluded, Social Security was "unsustainable."[43]

Once reelected to office in 2004, George W. Bush announced his intention to tackle these distant challenges. As he put it in his 2005 State of the Union address, "I recognize that [the future insolvency of Social Security] may seem a long way off. But those dates aren't so distant, as any parent will tell you." He then proposed a system of voluntary private investment accounts, which would be managed by the government, invested in private firms, and funded by a portion of the payroll tax that was going to fund the present system. This plan, he said, offered a way to prepare a twentieth-century social welfare program for the realities of the twenty-first century.[44]

Almost from the moment it was announced, the president's plan attracted intense scorn from major interest groups, Democratic politicians, and even some Republicans. Five days after Bush's second inaugural address, the American Association of Retired People (AARP), which endorsed Bush in the election, announced that it would oppose any plan that included private accounts. Democrats did not disabuse seniors of their anxiety at the thought of public funds being siphoned off into private accounts. Democratic National Committee chairman Howard Dean put it starkly:

"The president wants to take away our Social Security." As even right-leaning political observers noted, Democrats benefited politically—scoring points with seniors (and liberals)— simply by taking a strong stand against Bush's proposal. To gain from this battle, they did not need to come up with their own proposal for shoring up the financing of Social Security, which would inevitably have involved some combination of higher taxes and lower (or delayed) benefits—and thus political risk. And so they didn't. They offered no alternative.[45]

To be sure, Bush's plan was not perfect. Economists and advocates argued that the mechanism used to finance the private individual retirement accounts, at least in the short term, would accelerate the depletion of the Social Security fund. The White House also recognized that privatization alone would not solve the fiscal crisis of Social Security. In a memo, Bush political aide Peter Wehner acknowledged, "We simply cannot solve the Social Security problem with Personal Retirement Accounts alone. If the goal is permanent solvency and sustainability—as we believe it should be—then Personal Retirements Accounts, for all their virtues, are insufficient to that task." Wehner went on to state that major benefit cuts would be required.[46]

Nor was Bush an especially good salesman. Having invested so much political capital in this issue, Bush embarked on the first of what proved to be a long series of tours with public events at which he pitched his plan. This would prove an insurmountable challenge. Indeed, the more Bush talked about Social Security, the more support for his plan declined. In the months following the State of the Union address, public disapproval of Bush's handling of Social Security rose by sixteen points, from 48 percent to 64 percent.[47]

But here's the thing: while Bush floundered politically, not one of his plan's opponents made a concerted effort to address Social Security's long-term fiscal health. Instead, congressional leaders reflexively protected their own short-term interests. While Bush spoke about what America's fiscal state would look like in 2050, his counterparts in Congress fixated on the immediate downside risks of reform. And it did not help that in the coming midterm election, many of the young people who would ostensibly benefit from Bush's reform were expected to stay home while elderly Americans, who feared reform would endanger their own benefits, would reliably vote.[48] "Why stir up a political hornet's nest . . . when there is no urgency?" asked Republican Representative Rob Simmons, who was facing a competitive re-election. "When does the program go belly up? 2042. I will be dead by then."[49]

Failing to gain any political traction, in the spring of 2005 Bush took one last stab at Social Security reform. On April 28, in another effort to jump-start the debate, Bush embraced "progressive indexing," which would have protected low-wage workers and cut Social Security's projected shortfall. By statutory design, Social Security benefits increase over time based on a formula that takes into account both inflation and an index that averages the national increase in wages. Progressive indexing keeps that formula for the bottom 30 percent of wage earners, but for top-tier earners it calculates benefit increases by using inflation only. As Karl Rove put it, "Everyone would get a Social Security check equal to or greater in purchasing power than they would receive today, but low-wage earners would receive the more generous benefit increases the country could not afford for everyone. This one change would have eliminated roughly two-thirds of the Social Security shortfall."[50]

The president remained convinced that finding a solution to the program's long-term solvency problem was essential. "The temptation in Washington is to look at a major issue only in terms of whether it gives one political party an advantage over the other," he said. "Social Security is too important for 'politics as usual.' . . . [When a reform is agreed upon,] Republicans and Democrats will be able to stand together and take credit for doing what is right for our children and our grandchildren."[51] But his vision never materialized. Bush hoped that Social Security represented a departure from everyday partisan politics and re-election considerations. Unfortunately for him, Congress behaved as it always had.

No legislative version of his proposal even made it out of committee for a House vote. Nor did any other plausible solution to Social Security's long-term solvency issues. In lieu of private accounts and progressive indexing, members of Congress could have lowered Social Security benefits or raised the age of qualifying workers. It did neither. Indeed, as an institution, Congress managed to accomplish nothing at all.[52]

In his memoirs, Bush wrote that he did not regret taking on Social Security, insisting that he had taken a principled stand in support of the country's future. His ambitions were broader, and his vision extended further. As one journalist wrote during the president's tumultuous second term, Bush "often seems to also be talking directly to historians, tilting the pinball machine of presidential legacy." Bush's inability to enact Social Security reform was, perhaps, his most significant domestic policy defeat during his tenure as president. A central reason for his defeat was that he kept his sights on a different time horizon than did the members of Congress who stood in his way.[53]

Barack Obama Confronts the Dangers of Climate Change

The basic science on climate change is all but settled. The planet is heating up, humans bear some responsibility, and the medium- and long-term consequences could be devastating. The last two decades were the hottest in at least four hundred years. Hundreds of scientists operating under the banner of the Intergovernmental Panel on Climate Change concluded in 2007 that the warming climate was "more likely than not" caused by human activities. In 2013, the panel increased its certainty about the causal relationship, declaring it "extremely likely" that humans are responsible for the unprecedented temperature spike, and predicted catastrophic rises in sea levels. At this writing, 2015 is on track to be the hottest year on record—surpassing 2014, which is the current title holder. October 2015 was the hottest October ever recorded.[54]

While scientists nearly unanimously recognize the reality of climate change, much of the American public does not. Moreover, there are striking differences between Democrats and Republicans on the importance of the issue, and whether the government should play a role in solving it. Whereas many Democrats claim that climate change represents an urgent national (indeed global) problem that calls for a bold policy response by government and society, most Republicans reject both of these claims. Indeed, even those Republicans who recognize the science behind climate change nonetheless harbor serious concerns about the costs of government involvement.[55]

Although the parties vehemently disagree on this issue, as they do on many others that we examine in this book, the problem of climate change is not going away any time soon. We bring it up here not to promote the views of either party but to make sense of the striking differences that distinguish presidents from members of Congress on contentious matters of public policy. Presidents, regardless of their party, seek effective solutions to what they regard as pressing national problems. Congress, whichever party sits in control, is a bastion of special interests, favoritism, and localism. That is the story here. And that is why we tell it.

Because the science has mounted and converged over the last decade or so, and because the pressures for political action have mounted apace—not just in the United States but around the world—we focus our attention on how President Barack Obama responded, and what happened when he did. As a presidential candidate in 2008, Obama repeatedly expressed anxiety about the planet's future, and he pledged to act. To do so, Obama dusted off a policy that many Republicans had previously supported to reduce pollution: a market-based system of "cap and trade," in which annual limits for emissions would be set by the government, and firms could trade "allowances" to pollute. Following the advice of many economists, Obama recommended that initial allowances be auctioned off, just as the government had previously done for airwave rights. Subsequently, low-polluting firms that did not use all of their allowances would be permitted to sell their leftovers to high-polluting firms that had exhausted theirs. The result would be a system that recognized the different needs and capacities of firms while ensuring that target reductions in pollution were reached.

In a policy book released by his campaign during the election, Obama proposed a cap-and-trade system that he said would cut carbon emissions by 80 percent by 2050. "To ensure complete openness with the public and prevent unjustified corporate welfare, all allowances [to emit a given amount] will be auctioned," his campaign wrote.[56] Most revenues generated by the system would be used for rebates designed to lessen costs to the consumer. Obama also proposed requiring 10 percent of electricity to come from renewable sources by 2012 and investing $150 billion in clean technology which would create five million "green jobs."

In what looked to be an early legislative victory for the president, the House of Representatives in June 2009 passed the American Clean Energy and Security Act, or Waxman-Markey (after Representatives Henry Waxman and Edward Markey, the bill's authors), the first-ever legislation devoted to climate change. For the most part, Waxman-Markey faithfully represented Obama's plan. Its cap-and-trade system also aimed to cut emissions by 83 percent by 2050, with revenues largely going to aid consumers during the transition. And the president's involvement had much to do with the bill's passage. According to *Congressional Quarterly,* President Obama reached out to numerous members during the floor debate on the day of the vote. It passed on June 26, 219–212. According to a Waxman aide, "It would not have passed without the White House."[57]

Applauding the developments in the House, Obama appealed to a set of distinctly national considerations. At a June 2009 press conference, the president insisted that Waxman-Markey "will transform the way we produce and use energy in America. This legislation will spark a clean energy transformation that will reduce our dependence on foreign oil and confront the carbon pollution that threatens our planet." In the months that followed, the president pressed his case further. Climate change required national, transformative action of the sort that could not be achieved on a state-by-state basis. In his 2010 State of the Union speech, he argued that even doubters of the scientific consensus on global warming should support new legislation for the national economic benefits it would provide: "The nation that leads the clean energy economy will be the nation that leads the global economy. And America must be that nation." Obama then proclaimed in his 2011 budget (released in February 2010), "Failure to act [on climate change] jeopardizes our nation's security, our economy, and our future."[58]

In late 2009 and early 2010, all eyes were fixed on the Senate. There, Democrats John Kerry and Joe Lieberman and Republican Lindsey Graham led the charge for climate change legislation. After months of deal making with special interest groups, in May 2010 the three Senators finally unveiled their proposal, which ran around 1,000 pages. Kerry-Graham-Lieberman adopted many of Obama's core ideas about how to deal with climate change. Most important, by 2050 emissions would be cut by more than 80 percent. But while Obama's cap-and-trade system applied to the entire economy, this bill's plans would be phased in sector by sector. And whereas Obama wanted all allowances to be auctioned, Kerry-Graham-Lieberman *gave away* 75 percent of allowances for free—a boon to the (polluting) businesses most affected and a big drain on the revenue that would otherwise have been raised for consumers. Even this concession—and disruption to the bill's coherence—wasn't good enough for some of their counterparts. "It ought to be 100 percent," Democratic Senator Tom Harkin told the *New York Times*.[59]

Even after its sponsors made additional concessions to the Chamber of Commerce and major oil companies, though, the bill faced a gauntlet of opposition. Senators whose states depended heavily on coal for their electricity were deeply resistant to broad, costly changes. When Senator Lieberman, a Democrat, would meet with Senator Evan Bayh of Indiana to persuade him to sign on to the bill, Senator Bayh, also a Democrat, would respond by pointing to a US map. The map showed the extent to which his state relied on coal. Forty-nine percent of Indiana's electricity came from coal. "Every time Senator Lieberman would open his mouth, Bayh would show him the map," a Lieberman aide later told a reporter.[60]

Governor Joe Manchin's 2010 campaign for US Senate in the coal-heavy state of West Virginia featured an ad of him literally shooting a cap-and-trade bill. "It's bad for West Virginia," Manchin told the camera. Manchin was a Democrat. In total, forty-four House Democrats voted against Waxman-Markey. The states with the greatest number of Democratic opponents, Texas and Pennsylvania, ranked first and third among coal users.[61]

Lots of Democrats demanded state-specific provisions be inserted into the bill. Senator Blanche Lincoln of Arkansas sought protections for the major oil company in her state, Murphy Oil, which also happened to be one of Lincoln's top campaign contributors. Senator Debbie Stabenow of Michigan led a group of Democrats from farm-heavy states in an effort to please agriculture. She introduced a companion bill that would regulate the cap-and-trade "offsets" system. Offsets meant lucrative credits for the cap-and-trade market, ostensibly given to firms that engaged in environmentally desirable activity. Stabenow's bill, however, would grant offsets to private activities of dubious environmental merit, such as tree-cutting and pesticide-spraying. Additionally, agriculture-related offsets would be decided by the United States Department of Agriculture, not the more fearsome EPA. Unsurprisingly, industry welcomed Stabenow's efforts. The National Milk Producers Federation praised her and her three Senate Democrat allies for "creating revenue opportunities."[62]

Piece by piece, Kerry-Graham-Lieberman was watered down to placate industry and regional concerns. The emissions reduction target remained the same as the president's, but the cap-and-trade system was different, designed to accommodate industry demands. Many allowances would be given away, not sold. There was nary a mention of green job investments along the lines of what Obama had initially wanted. To win industry support, the bill actually removed regulatory power from the EPA while overriding states' existing efforts to regulate emissions. No effort was spared to win industry and bipartisan support, and the resulting bill was a faint approximation of what Obama initially proposed.

By late 2010, it was clear that Kerry-Graham-Lieberman would not pass the Senate. Cap and trade came to be seen as a new tax, and senators did not want to be viewed as imposing an additional tax in a challenged economy.[63] Whatever the faults of the Obama White House, however, many senators shared the wisdom of Joe Manchin. Cap and trade was not good for *their* state, and thus not worth pursuing. Its vices and virtues for the nation as a whole—and for the planet—did not matter nearly so much.

After being reelected and seeing Democrats lose the House in 2012, Obama turned to the only recourse available: executive action. The Climate Action Plan announced in June 2013 promised loan guarantees for fossil fuel projects, directed agencies to develop strategies for reducing methane emissions, established longer-term plans for reducing carbon pollution, and did a good deal more besides. Even so, the plan was a picture of diminished ambition. Congress was not mentioned, and the goal of using cap and trade to reduce emissions—a goal that the president had articulated and the congressional bills had supported—was gone. The soaring rhetoric and substantive commitment of the president had run into the buzz saw of partisanship and regionalism.[64]

And still, the president pressed onward. In August 2015, Obama announced a batch of regulations meant to combat climate change, including, most ambitiously, the reduction of greenhouse gas emissions from power plants by 32 percent from 2005 levels. He did so, the *New York Times* argued, "with his legacy in mind." In a speech announcing the new regulations, Obama insisted that "no challenge poses a greater threat to our future and future generations than a changing climate." And should we fail to meet it, Obama said, our children and grandchildren will rightfully condemn us. "We're the last generation that can do something" about climate change, and if we fail to meet this challenge, the president warned, future generations will appropriately judge us with contempt.[65]

For their part, members of Congress responded just as we have come to expect. Led by representatives of coal-producing states, notably Mitch McConnell (R-KY), members voiced all sorts of opposition to the president's plans. For them, this remained a fight about jobs and businesses back home—plain and simple. "In Kentucky, these regulations would likely mean fewer jobs, shuttered power plants, higher electricity costs for families and businesses," McConnell intoned. "I'm not going to sit by while the White House takes aims at the life blood of our state's economy. I'm going to keep doing everything I can to fight them."[66] And fight them he did, plotting court challenges, coordinating with state attorneys general, and encouraging state governors to resist the president's demands.

During his two terms in office, Obama went well beyond these domestic initiatives in his quest to tackle climate change. He also launched international initiatives aimed at rallying the world to action. At the 2009 Copenhagen Summit, he prodded nearly two dozen countries to agree to nonbinding emission cuts. That accord was initially welcomed by key members of Congress. An aide to Republican senator Richard Lugar called it a "home run," and Republican senator Lisa Murkowski labeled it "progress." Before long, however, both senators distanced themselves from legislation seeking to bind the US to such cuts, which failed. And while Obama went on to engage foreign nations on climate change— leading to the 2015 Paris climate agreement—Congress continues to stand in the way of the implementation of any agreement brokered on the international stage.[67]

Throughout this long saga, the president and Congress conformed to the roles in which they had been cast. With a broader and longer view, Obama sought solutions to a problem that threatens not just the nation but the globe. In so doing, he gave shorter shrift to the immediate needs and wants of local communities. Their interests, instead, found voice in Congress. It was no accident, moreover, that the legislators who worked hardest on the issue of climate change did so on behalf of the coal and gas industries on which their local economies depended—and are the worst polluters.

Lessons

In the case studies surveyed in this chapter, we find a diverse assembly of presidents. They represented very different ideological orientations. They came to office under very different circumstances. They enjoyed very different levels of support within Congress and the broader public. But as presidents, they all embodied a set of commitments and values that run in short supply on Capitol Hill: they approached policy from a national perspective, they sought policy solutions that would be effective and durable over the long term, and they took responsibility for government and policy as a whole and sought to bring greater coherence to them.

These features are built into the office of presidency. All presidents possess them, whatever their party, whatever their ideology, whatever their specific policy agendas—and these are the features that make presidential leadership so promising and valuable. As individuals, presidents may be astoundingly different in personality, background, and most everything else that might seem to bear on their governing behavior. What exactly does Barack Obama have in common with Dwight Eisenhower? Not much. But personal differences are mostly beside the point. What matters is that, as presidents, their incentives are structured in much the same way—and as a result, they can both be expected to behave *presidentially*. All presidents can. They are all wired the same. And that is a good thing for the nation.

Yet this good thing is being squandered. When trying to advance comprehensive change, presidents rarely emerge triumphant. They are underpowered in the American system of government, and they usually cannot even come close to achieving their objectives. This often happens because Congress simply refuses to take up their legislative initiatives. But it also happens even when presidents "win"— for most often they can expect Congress to load up their policy initiatives with special deals for key members, to dilute key provisions, and to carve out exceptions and loopholes for favored industries, yielding "designs" that are ill-suited to actually solving the problems they are supposed to be addressing.

We aren't saying that presidents always get things right. They (and their advisers) can suffer lapses of judgment and pursue policies that are poorly crafted or unwise. Had Bush's efforts to privatize Social Security succeeded, who knows what further damage the Great Recession would have inflicted on the domestic economy, not to mention the nation's social safety net. It could have been a disaster for seniors. Yet Bush was right in drawing the nation's attention to the long-term solvency of Social Security and insisting on a coherent policy solution. He was doing precisely what a leader ought to be doing, and what the nation needs. Congress, in this case, was right to criticize Bush's policy solutions—but it was wrong and irresponsible to then ignore the problem he properly identified, and wrong and irresponsible not to offer a serious alternative solution and then act on it.

So this is where the rubber meets the road. If the nation is to get serious about solving its pressing social problems, it *must* look to presidential leadership, not to Congress. That doesn't mean that all checks and balances should somehow be abandoned. Nor does it mean that local interests and short-term concerns should be entirely forsaken. But it does mean that presidents need to play a much stronger role in American government.

4

Toward a More Effective Government

The Constitution is a relic of the past. It was devised by the founders some 225 years ago for a simple agrarian society, and the form of government they settled upon, a separation-of-powers system with a parochial Congress at its center, was perhaps appropriate for their times. But it is not appropriate for our times. It is grossly out of sync with the requirements of modern society and egregiously incapable of dealing with the formidable array of serious social problems that arise in the modern era.

How can the nation move toward a more effective government? What reforms are likely to work? As a starting point, it is important to resist platitudes about democracy always being complicated and messy, progress inevitably being slow and incremental, or the current political order being the best we can reasonably hope for. That kind of inside-the-box thinking—which is all too common among even the most sophisticated observers of American politics—embraces the status quo. A little soul-searching reveals that it is based on an implicit assumption that the Constitution is off limits, and thus an iron cage that evermore constrains not just our actions but our very imaginings about what is possible.

But the Constitution can't be off limits—because it is the problem. It makes democracy much more complicated and much messier than it needs to be. It makes progress much slower and more haphazard. It limits the kind of political order that we can craft for ourselves to meet our own needs as a modern nation. And it does these things because it is outdated. The solution is not to submit to it and look everywhere else for things to reform—like campaign finance or lobbying or party primaries or gerrymandering. Such efforts may help at the margins, but they don't get to the root of the problem. The root of the problem is an outdated Constitution—and the solution is to update it so that it better squares with the requirements of modern times.

How can this be accomplished? A dreamer might envision swapping a presidential for a parliamentary system, or in other ways scrapping the Constitution's original design and starting over from scratch to build something entirely new. But that really *is* dreaming. Nothing of the sort is in the realm of possibility. And a massive redesign would be way too risky and dangerous anyway. The reality is that, going forward, most aspects of the American constitutional system—its separated and federated powers, its two-chamber Congress, its independent judiciary—will remain the same and must be taken as given, warts and all. That said, targeted reforms can still be successful, and indeed, if rightly chosen, they can transform the way the system as a whole operates and performs. And that is the key to progress. The proponents of reform need to be bold, by putting the Constitution itself in their sights, but also pragmatic, by singling out specific changes that promise to have the biggest payoffs for effective government, are low in risk, and stand a reasonable chance of actually being adopted.

What might these changes look like? By now, the answer should be apparent: the most promising way to move our governmental system in the right direction is by amplifying the powers of the presidency. Presidents have built-in institutional incentives that propel them to be champions of effective government. And with their abiding attention to the national interest, their drive to achieve long-term policy solutions to national problems, and their focus on the integrity of the whole of government, presidents provide an absolutely crucial counterweight to the pathologies of Congress—and offer precisely the kind of performance-driven leadership the nation so desperately needs. If the Constitution is to be updated, then, and if limited, targeted, practical reforms are of the essence, the presidency is the place to look.

More specifically, presidents should be granted enhanced agenda-setting powers to propose bills to Congress, which Congress should then be required to vote on without amendment, on a strictly majoritarian basis, within a fixed period of time. This is the way "fast-track authority" currently works in the realm of international trade—when Congress has chosen to grant presidents that authority—and many years of experience show that it works quite well to promote coherent, well-integrated outcomes in that realm precisely because Congress is not allowed to fiddle with the policy's contents. The difference here is that the Constitution would be amended to grant the president *permanent* fast-track authority over *all* policy matters (including budgets and appointments). The president would propose. Congress would decide, up or down. Both would participate in the policy process—but the balance of power would shift in the president's direction, and presidential leadership would be unleashed to play a far greater role in promoting coherent, effective policy outcomes for the nation.

Let us be clear: this is *not* an argument for an imperial presidency. Congress and the courts would remain in place, and they would continue to impose important checks on presidential actions. Congress, moreover, would continue to express the local concerns of districts and states. The heart of the reform, then, has nothing to do with gutting the Constitution and somehow making the president all-powerful. On the contrary, it simply installs a somewhat different way of doing business—one that the nation already has a lot of positive experience with. Congress and the president would both be involved in the making of public policy, as they are now. But under this reform, Congress would be made less central to the policy process and the president more central. Presidential leadership and the qualities it promotes would thus be assigned a much more prominent role in American government.

WHERE THE PRESIDENT NOW SITS

How do the laws get written today? For the most part, the same way they always have. Congress (and all of its pathologies) sits in the driver's seat, while the presidency (and all its promise) is relegated to the back seat. If our government is going to get serious about solving problems, these seat assignments need to be reversed.

The Congress we live with today is the first branch of government, at least when it comes to writing laws. Members of Congress decide which problems warrant a legislative response, and these same members select which solutions, if any, will be open for consideration, what kinds of amendments will be allowed, what the substantive content of all this will actually be, and how the voting will proceed. And if a national problem divides their partisan loyalties or threatens their parochial interests or presents some inconvenience to the lobbyists who back them, members of Congress need not cook up some grand and principled explanation for refusing to address it. They can just set it aside and carry on with their business. They are the gatekeepers of the nation's laws.

To be sure, people outside of Congress can and do attempt to influence the goings-on within it. Lobbyists of every imaginable description descend upon Congress to register their pleas and press for action; constituencies large and small do the same, often in less-organized but still very vocal ways; and for electoral reasons alone, members have ample reasons to listen. Journalists put Congress under a bright spotlight, subjecting it to constant scrutiny and asking persistent questions about how it intends to react to vexing social problems. Constitutionally, however, members of Congress are quite on their own. They are the ones in authority, and no one outside of Congress can force its members to introduce, vote on, or pass legislation. They, and they alone, get to decide whether new bills are introduced to tackle tax reform, immigration, or any other matter of public consequence. And if you don't like what they propose, when they propose it, how they defend it, or the fact that they do not propose anything at all, well, tough. They cannot be compelled to do what they don't want to do. And if they decide to open the gates and act, whatever they cobble together as the content of the law is what the public is going to get.

Presidents, more than anyone, provide a corrective to this state of affairs. They are constitutionally relegated to the back seat of government, but they have never accepted this as their political lot in life. Especially since the Progressive years, presidents have pushed hard to put themselves in the driver's seat—and to accumulate as much power as possible to make it happen. Their power remains wholly insufficient for them to truly lead. But they have taken great strides over the decades and in many respects have presidentialized the political system—from the back seat.

As a result, modern presidents have been reasonably successful, constitutional authority or no, at setting Congress's policy agenda. With Theodore Roosevelt blazing the trail, they have found ways to impress their ideas, their convictions, and their policy priorities upon the American polity—by meeting regularly with the press, for example, fully deploying the powers of their bully pulpit, and "going public" to rivet the nation's attention on specific policy reforms.[1] And with Congress so fragmented and incapable of coherent action, presidents have seized the opportunity to simplify and crystallize the policy options for all concerned. Harry Truman was the first president to begin submitting a legislative program to Congress every year—and when Eisenhower assumed office and initially failed to do so, he was roundly castigated by members of Congress, including those in his own party, who valued the focus presidents were providing them. His administration quickly fell into step by putting this Truman-designed institutional capacity to use, and from that point on all modern presidents, regardless of party, have routinely submitted their legislative programs to Congress—and those programs have essentially set Congress's policy agenda. This has been a major step in presidentializing the system, and in simply bringing it a measure of order, coherence, and leadership.

As it takes up the president's policy agenda, Congress actually makes the laws, of course, and determines their specific contents. But presidents have the formal authority to veto and that gives them additional leverage within the legislative process itself, because legislators need to worry all along about what the president will or will not accept. This dynamic allows presidents to extract concessions from Congress on some bills, stop others in their tracks, hurry others along—and throughout, deploy a small army of White House staffers to lobby individual members of Congress, coordinate and haggle with party leaders, engage in pork-barrel politics, and otherwise get as much presidential policy adopted as possible, hopefully in a form that is at least dimly recognizable. In 2015, for example, the nation saw its president—a lame duck, and thus in a weak bargaining position—wage intensive and protracted congressional lobbying campaigns on the Iran nuclear deal, the Trans-Pacific Partnership, the thawing of relations with Cuba, immigration reform, and America's Clean Power Plan (on climate change). Presidents are hardly bystanders. Yet for all their efforts in the legislative process—which are considerable and relentless—they are profoundly weakened by the basic constitutional reality: they cannot compel Congress to take any action at all, and when Congress does act, they cannot control the contents of the bills that get enacted.[2]

Presidents have also been driven, as discussed, to expand their powers outside the halls of Congress, allowing them to shape the nation's laws (including their implementation) in ways that don't directly involve the passage of bills. A principal means by which they have done this is by building up—sometimes with congressional assistance—their own institutional capacity for action. This has involved creating all sorts of administrative units, including the Office of Management and Budget, the National Security Council, the Council of Economic Advisers, White House committees and councils for policymaking, presidential offices for legislative liaison and appointments, the Office of Information and Regulatory Affairs, the Office of Personnel Management, the larger Executive Office of the President (in which these and many other presidential agencies are housed), and more.[3] These many units, which make up the institutional presidency, give presidents much-needed information, advice, and institutional memory, just as they help the president shape policy ideas, coordinate the various components of government, control the bureaucracy, and put presidential discretion to effective use. The institutional presidency is the president's prime means of trying to impose coherent order, and make coherent policy, in a nation where separation of powers and Congress make those goals almost impossible to achieve. This institutional capacity is insufficient. But it is a counterweight to the otherwise leaderless cacophony of parochial voices in American politics.

Along with these institutional mechanisms, presidents have another important avenue for shaping the nation's laws: the strategic use of executive orders, executive agreements, national security directives, and proclamations. With these unilateral powers, presidents have advanced all manner of policy changes, many of which would never have survived the legislative process. From Jefferson's expansion of US territory with the Louisiana Purchase to Lincoln's freeing of the slaves with the Emancipation Proclamation to Truman's desegregation of the military to Clinton's protection of millions of acres of federal lands as national monuments to Bush's provision of federal funding for faith-based initiatives to Obama's raising of the minimum wage for federal contract workers, presidents of both parties have made the most of their unilateral powers.[4] Presidents, moreover, do not merely exercise these unilateral powers. They nourish them, they adapt them to suit their needs, and sometimes they invent them anew. Given the legislative minefield awaiting them in Congress, successive presidents have worked mightily to build an arsenal of unilateral policy tools that allow them to venture forth into policy domains where Congress refuses to tread. It is no exaggeration to say that the president's capacity to make policy unilaterally—and to do so with only rare reversals from Congress or the courts—constitutes a defining feature of the modern presidency. At the end of the day, however, unilateral actions are no substitute for laws. The kind of sweeping, coordinated, and holistic change that many policy challenges demand can only come through legislative action. Lacking either statutory or constitutional authority, presidents can muster only a rough facsimile of what is actually needed.

Presidents have worked tirelessly to meet the expansive expectations that the American public has thrust upon them. And in various ways—setting the policy agenda, directly engaging in the legislative process, building and deploying the institutional presidency, and taking unilateral action—they have enhanced their power and asserted their distinctive voice. Constitutionally, however, each president continues to work from a place of weakness. At nearly every turn, he confronts legislators who have preeminent formal authority in the making of the nation's laws and a legislative process that makes it virtually impossible to generate coherent, effective policies. The president can reach out to members of Congress, but they have no obligation to follow his lead. He can set their agenda, but they have no obligation to enact it or even vote on it. And if they do bring something to a vote, it is likely to be a cobbled-together creation that is but a pale reflection of what the president actually wanted.

Why has Congress done nothing over the last decade to reform the nation's immigration system, a reform actively pursued by both George W. Bush and Barack Obama? Why did Congress fail to adopt anything even remotely resembling a policy that would address the nation's hugely consequential dependence on foreign oil, when presidents of both parties were aggressively pushing for a strong energy policy? Why did Congress fail to take any action, over some seventy years, as president after president, Democrat and Republican alike, pushed for moves toward universal health care? And why, when health-care reform was finally adopted, did it turn out to be such a grotesque design grafted onto the existing system without serious attention to cost concerns? In these and other cases, the answers are all the same: Congress is wired to produce ineffective, inadequate responses to the nation's pressing social problems—and presidents, even as they try to offer a corrective, must operate in a system that is stacked against them.

This cannot go on. If we are to meet the challenges that our country now faces, the system must be changed. We need to put the president at the helm. Congress must continue, of course, to play a vital role in representing local interests, monitoring and evaluating the president's plans for the country, and giving its consent to public policy. And presidents must be constrained—for as is true of all political actors, they cannot always be trusted to do what is right, and they are bound to make mistakes. But when it comes to setting the agenda, crafting coherent policies, and taking the lead in addressing the nation's problems, it is the president—not Congress—who should be the nation's steward.

SOMETHING TO BUILD UPON: FAST-TRACK AUTHORITY

As we've already noted, a practical way to harness the advantages of presidential leadership is through a simple expansion of the fast-track authority that, for several decades, Congress and the president have put to use many times in making decisions on international trade agreements. By way of background, let's take a brief look at what the experience has been.

The United States, as the world's leading economy, is affected by the economies of nations throughout the world, and over the past century it has been actively involved in negotiating all manner of trade agreements—from small bilateral agreements with single nations to huge multilateral agreements with many nations, such as the General Agreement on Tariffs and Trade (GATT). When the president attempts to negotiate these agreements, he must navigate enormous complexities involving large numbers and types of industries and commodities, diverse impacts on multiple business and social constituencies, pressing concerns about labor and environmental regulations, nagging domestic political considerations, and the panoply of demands and constraints weighing on their negotiating partners. Any trade agreement, once arrived at, consists of many, many intricately interconnected parts on which negotiating parties were ultimately able to converge. It is a coherent, well-integrated whole.

On the American side, these agreements are hammered out and crafted by teams of trade experts from the federal bureaucracy under the authoritative guidance of the president. The president is responsible for making these agreements happen, he is responsible for their contents, and he is responsible for ensuring that they best promote the national interest. This is the only practical way that such trade agreements can be achieved—Congress is obviously in no position to negotiate them—and this is how it has been done throughout the modern era, when the United States has played such a prominent role on the international scene. It makes sense.

But here is the problem. Trade agreements, as we've said, are coherent, well-integrated packages that have been laboriously put together through negotiations with other nations. Yet if these agreements need to be adopted by Congress as laws through the usual legislative process, there is nothing to keep legislators from doing what they routinely do with all presidential proposals: namely, diving headlong into the details, objecting to provisions that threaten special interests and constituencies, insisting on new provisions that protect or promote the interests they want to favor, and otherwise scrambling, rearranging, and blowing holes in what began as a coherent policy. Were Congress to engage in lawmaking as it normally does, then, trade agreements would rarely make it through the legislative gauntlet—and whatever emerged would not be what the nations involved had originally agreed to and would nullify the negotiators' efforts. Worse, any nations the United States tried to negotiate with would anticipate this sort of congressional meddling and nullification from the outset and recognize that the negotiators were not actually speaking for the United States and could not make commitments, and the whole enterprise of negotiating international treaties would break down.

Such an outcome would obviously be disastrous. The nation, therefore, has settled on two basic ways to avoid it. The first is that presidents have relied heavily on their powers of unilateral action. While the Constitution requires that treaties be ratified by two-thirds of the Senate before becoming law, presidents long ago— during the 1800s—began calling certain negotiated arrangements with other nations "executive agreements" that had the same force of law as treaties but did not need to go through Congress, and the Supreme Court eventually gave its explicit consent.[5] This presidential maneuver obviously removed a huge political barrier to international trade negotiations, and modern presidents have found it enormously attractive. Whereas nineteenth-century presidents issued just a handful of executive agreements each year, today they run into the hundreds, constituting the overwhelming majority of international agreements involving the American government.

At times, however, the president has no choice but to go to Congress—usually because the deal in question is so consequential, economically and politically, that the president faces a political firestorm if he doesn't make Congress a partner in legitimizing the arrangement. Landmark trade agreements like the North American Free Trade Agreement (NAFTA) nearly always take the form of a treaty, not an executive agreement. The same often applies for agreements that involve especially well-organized and well-funded industries.

How, then, can the nation allow Congress to participate in treaty-making—on the most important of international agreements, no less—and avoid the kind of disaster that Congress is wired to produce? The answer is that the nation's leaders have relied upon a novel way of getting Congress involved, one that departs from the usual legislative process but still allows Congress to pass judgment on whatever agreements have been negotiated. The solution they hit upon involves granting the president fast-track authority.

Under the fast-track model, originally set out in the 1974 Trade Act, the president delivers to Congress a fully formed proposal and its members must render a singular verdict, yes or no. Neither the House nor the Senate can offer any amendments, and members are thus enjoined from reconsidering or rewriting the terms of the trade agreement. They also must act within a reasonably short period of time, with committees allotted a maximum of forty-five days to evaluate the treaty, after which it is automatically discharged. The floor is then given a maximum of fifteen days to vote. Floor debate, moreover, is limited to twenty hours in each chamber, voting must proceed on a strictly majoritarian basis, and the Senate cannot filibuster.[6]

With fast track, Congress can no longer substitute inaction for opposition, for if its members fail to vote within the defined period of time, the terms of the president's bill—whatever they are—automatically become law. And because voting proceeds on an up-or-down basis with no amendments, the president can present Congress with a coherent, well-integrated policy proposal that will not be altered, distorted, or gutted as Congress considers it. With fast-track authority, the president becomes the proposer of public policy—and he is also the one who crafts its contents, which he knows will be preserved.

Congress remains an integral part of the decision process. Should the president put before its members a particularly misguided trade proposal, they retain all the authority they need to strike it down. And if they do that, the president faces the uncomfortable decision—and likely, the political humiliation—of either scrapping the deal entirely or returning to his trade partners and setting to work on new terms. So at every step along the way, as the trade agreement is being assembled, the president has strong incentives to anticipate what Congress is willing to accept and to craft his proposal with that in mind. Even with the president firmly ensconced in the front seat, then, the outcome is very much a joint product and not one that is somehow imposed by the executive.

Presidents have not always had fast-track authority. Indeed, the legislative history of fast-track authority has been rocky, with partisan considerations sometimes playing a role in determining whether Congress would or would not grant it. Economically, the United States opened itself to the world with the 1934 Reciprocal

Trade Agreement Act, the first time that Congress granted the president broad authority to negotiate tariff reforms—although the legislative process for gaining congressional approval remained the same.[7] Forty years later, with the 1974 Trade Act, a Democratic Congress took the big additional step of giving the sitting Republican president, Richard Nixon, temporary fast-track authority—and, more generally, setting up and authorizing (for a specific, limited period of time) the fast-track model of decision-making on trade agreements. The act was an explicit effort to reduce the influence of special interests on international negotiations and to strengthen the president's ability to credibly bargain with foreign states. With several extensions, Gerald Ford and then his successors, both Republican and Democrat, held this authority for the better part of twenty years, during which time they successfully used the fast-track model to win congressional passage of bilateral free trade agreements with Japan, Israel, and Canada, as well as the regional North American Free Trade Agreement.

When Republicans took over the House in 1995 and sought to reassert congressional control, they allowed fast-track authority to lapse. As long as Bill Clinton sat in office, they showed little penchant for renewing it. Under pressure from newly elected George W. Bush, however, members of Congress resuscitated the power in 2002—which allowed him, subsequently, to win congressional passage of bilateral agreements with Chile, Singapore, Australia, Morocco, Peru, and other countries. Although the power lapsed once again in 2007, Bush and then Obama continued to deploy the option on those negotiations that were already under way (as the previous law allowed), enabling them to finalize agreements with Colombia, South Korea, and Panama and still use fast track to win congressional passage.[8]

The spring of 2015 saw a huge potential trade agreement be-tween the United States and nations around the Pacific Rim looming on the horizon, giving rise to another push for renewed fast-track authority. This time, it was achieved through an odd but productive pattern of bipartisanship: after many congressional Democrats—fearing for American jobs and in a protectionist mood—abandoned their own president in his push for fast track, the Republican-con-trolled Senate passed legislation giving Obama the authority he sought. This victory allowed him to pursue a massive trade agree-ment with eleven Asian nations that would create the Trans-Pacific Partnership, a free-trade area expected to be greatly beneficial to the nations involved, but also to serve as a buffer against Chinese eco-nomic expansion. The 2015 extension of fast-track authority also allowed the president to pursue the Transatlantic Trade and Invest-ment Partnership with Europe. Both deals would lower tariffs, ex-pand trade, and create new regulations for sectors as diverse as agriculture, banking, and the pharmaceutical industry. This latest grant of fast-track authority holds for six years.[9]

What have the last forty years taught us about the advantages of fast-track authority? Two things above all else. First, it has al-lowed the United States to take an active role in arranging major trade agreements that otherwise would almost surely not have been possible, and to get those agreements passed into law with the consent of Congress. The nation's trade negotiators, backed by presidential fast-track authority, had the power to make meaning-ful and credible commitments to other nations. Presidents did not have to end-run Congress by using executive agreements. And in the end, policies designed to be genuinely coherent, effective, and forward-looking—because they were crafted by presidents—were endorsed by *both* presidents and Congress in a joint decision process that required mutual consent. This is what a process of effective policymaking looks like.

Second, fast-track authority has allowed the national interest to take priority over narrow special interests. Congress is a boiling cauldron of protectionism, with powerful groups of every imaginable stripe taking aim at each provision of each trade agreement and pressing for changes that would work to their own special advantage, regardless of the impact on the nation. It is the president, not Congress, who insists on trade policies that best promote the national interest—and these are usually policies that expand trade, are not protectionist, and rise above special-interest pressures. In a University of Chicago Booth School of Business poll of economists from around the globe, fully 85 percent affirm the view that "freer trade improves productive efficiency and offers consumers better choices, and in the long run these gains are much larger than any effects on employment." Yes, particular industries and workers may be disadvantaged. And yes, some agreements are better crafted than others. But overall, economists overwhelmingly agree, expanded trade has led to higher economic growth, lower consumer prices, and a dramatic expansion of available goods and services. In view of that, it is not surprising that *all* modern presidents, Democrat as well as Republican, have favored the pursuit of trade-expanding agreements with other nations.[10]

In and of itself, of course, fast-track authority does not prescribe a particular policy course but simply introduces a different, more effective model of joint decision-making that puts the president in the front seat. It is because of the president's unique outlook—one that eschews parochialism in favor of the national interest—that presidential leadership under fast track has been used to expand free trade. Were prime authority placed in the hands of legislators instead, we could expect all kinds of protections and aid to flow to special-interest constituencies, if indeed trade agreements could actually be reached. Authority does not make policy. The officeholder who exercises it does, and the policy is shaped and determined by the incentives structuring that officeholder's behavior. It is because the president is driven to represent the nation as a whole that successive presidents from both parties have used this authority to expand free markets around the globe. Fast-track authority has allowed them to do that very effectively— and to overcome special-interest pressures in winning congressional consent.[11]

OUR PROPOSAL

Fast-track authority is not a leap into the unknown. It is familiar and well tested. Presidents and Congress have had forty years of positive experience with it, they know how it works, and they know how to operate according to its rules. The decision model it introduces, moreover, moves our government in precisely the right direction: by putting the president in the driver's seat, it gives priority to the national interest, allows for the crafting of coherent policies, and enhances the government's capacity to take effective action.

So far, fast-track authority has only been used in the realm of trade policy, and only when Congress has chosen to make it available. What we are proposing is that fast-track authority be made permanent and that it apply to all policies. This, essentially, is the entire reform. Simple as that. The details, such as they are, are those we just discussed: the president would have the right to craft a complete policy and propose it to Congress, Congress would be required to take an up-or-down vote without amendment within a specified period of time, and the vote in each chamber would be on a majoritarian basis (no filibuster).[12] If Congress failed to follow these steps to a final vote, the president's proposal would become law without Congress's consent.

This reform would require a constitutional amendment, as it would clearly introduce a fundamental change to the way policy decisions for the nation are made. But this change also is very simple, very limited, and very pragmatic. *The rest of the Constitution would stay exactly the same.* Separation of powers would remain. Congress and the courts would remain. Federalism would remain. The Bill of Rights would remain. The only difference is that something new would be added: fast-track authority.

In the absence of reform, the Constitution renders it virtually impossible for the nation to have effective government. By putting Congress at the center of the legislative process, it ensures that Congress's pathologies will infect all of public policy, and indeed the entire governmental system. These pathologies are not going to be remedied unless Congress is pushed into the back seat, where it belongs. Fast track does that. This is one of its most powerful advantages as a targeted reform. Even so, fast track is also a limited reform—by design—and Congress would continue to play important representational roles in the system. Above all, no presidential proposal could become law without Congress's consent (assuming it voted in time, according to the rules)—and that is a very big role indeed. The president would be in no position to simply ramrod his proposals through. He would hardly be a dictator, indifferent to congressional preferences. If members of Congress were opposed to his proposal, they could simply vote it down. Presidents, therefore, would need to craft and propose policies that could ultimately gain the consent of Congress.

Congress, moreover, would continue to have the authority under the Constitution to pass whatever laws it wants—subject, of course, to a presidential veto. Legislators, then, could continue to go about their business of addressing the needs of local constituencies and special-interest groups. They also would be free to offer alternatives to the president's policy proposals and thereby avoid being boxed in by the president. That members of Congress retain such legislative authority is not only practical but also a good thing, for presidents are less likely to notice or care about local concerns; and if these concerns are to get a hearing and find expression in American national politics, their more steadfast defenders in Congress need to be able to introduce and pursue bills of their own. And so they can.

The bottom line is that, under this expansion of fast track, Congress could largely do what it has always done. It could try to pass its own bills. It could try to respond to special interests and constituencies. And its consent would be necessary if any proposal is to become law. But the brute fact is, Congress wouldn't have as much power or centrality, and it would play a subordinate role to the president. As a result, its pathologies would remain—but they would be marginalized and wouldn't do as much damage.

Under fast track, presidents would have much more than the right to make proposals to Congress. They have that right already. They would have the right to require that their proposals be considered by Congress under the fast-track decision model—which means that Congress would be forced to vote up or down on the precise policy package that the president proposes, without change. With that decision model in operation, backed by their formal authority to veto (if they choose) whatever Congress tries to do on its own, presidents would be in a far better position to get the policies they want with the precise content they want. They would have true agenda control, and they can be expected to use it to the hilt.

As they do so, they will use it to promote effective government. Presidents already have strong incentives to seek policies that are coherent, well-integrated, well-designed solutions to pressing national problems—for these are precisely the kinds of policies they need to achieve during their terms of office in order to establish their legacies as great leaders. What fast-track authority will do, then, is give presidents the authority they need to design policies in the most effective possible ways, knowing that Congress cannot reach in to alter the contents. Congress will have to vote on policies just as presidents have crafted them. Presidents will need to anticipate what majorities in Congress will actually vote for, of course, and they will not be able to ignore congressional preferences and hope to succeed legislatively. But presidential agenda power will be enormous. And by being able to eliminate other policy alternatives that some members of Congress might favor—because presidents can successfully veto most anything Congress does—and by ensuring that their policies offer at least something to a majority of legislators (as opposed to the nothing they would get by voting no), presidents will be in an excellent position to get Congress's consent.

Fast track has worked very well for presidents in international trade, as they have used it to get their negotiated agreements through Congress. And much the same is likely to happen across other policy realms. Agenda control is a powerful thing, and in this case, it is harnessed to presidential leadership—and to the national interest and effective government—through a simple, straightforward reform that leaves almost the entirety of the Constitution firmly in place. The risks are low. The promise, extraordinary. The costs of doing nothing—devastating.

Details, Qualifications, and a Reality Check

Expanding fast-track authority to cover more than just trade is not so much inventing a new presidential power as leveraging an existing one. It leverages that power, moreover, in ways that put the president's strengths where they are needed most, while still maintaining vital congressional checks and oversight. Still, legitimate questions arise about the efficacy and practicality of our proposed reform. And so here, we offer some brief responses.

Why not fix Congress instead? We are hardly the first to recognize the pathologies of Congress as an institution. Pragmatic concerns about the capacity of our Congress-centric government to solve problems have a long and storied intellectual history. It is not too surprising, then, that in contemporary politics would-be political reformers see Congress as the main source of the system's dysfunction and reforms of Congress and elections as the best way to make the system functional again. There is no shortage of books that first disparage Congress and then call for its redemption. By restricting the activities of lobbyists on Capitol Hill, reducing the flow of money through Congress, reforming party primaries, clamping down on gerrymandering, or encouraging legislators to rediscover their institutional identities, it is thought, a more effective government will be returned to the American people. Strengthening the presidency, meantime, is rarely part of the reform discussion at all.[13]

We too have our favored congressional reforms. How about eliminating the Senate filibuster? But these sorts of reforms don't really get to the root of the problem, and they distract from the fundamentals that need to be center stage. Those who would invest their hopes in Congress—and ignore the presidency in the process—too often hold out hope that, with the right reforms, American government can return to the good old days when legislators could overcome their differences and enact reams of effective legislation. As we have said all along, however, there were no good old days. Congress has never been good at addressing the nation's problems, and its pathologies are wired into it by a Constitution written more than two hundred years ago.

By constitutional design, Congress is a two-chamber decision-making body that comprises hundreds of elected officials from local jurisdictions, all seeking their own political welfare in their own ways. Parochialism is woven into the warp and woof of the institution, and policy change, when it occurs, tends to be weak and incoherent and to proceed with little care for how the pieces fit into a larger, well-working whole. To transform Congress into an effective problem-solver for the nation would require institutional reforms far more drastic than any of its devotees are willing to recommend. Eliminating district and state jurisdictions in favor of national ones, for instance, might do the trick. But the changes wrought to Congress would be so radical as to render the institution unrecognizable—and the realities of American politics would never allow for such a radical amendment to the Constitution anyway.

As a practical matter, then, the fundamental source of Congress's pathologies cannot be reached through reform. The solution is not to pretend that other types of reforms—to campaign finance and all the rest—will somehow do the job, because they won't. The solution, rather, is to accept the fact that Congress will continue to behave pretty much as it always has, and to pursue reforms that simply make Congress less central to the nation's decision process, and thus make its pathologies less consequential.

That is precisely what fast track does—by moving Congress from the front seat to the back seat of government.

Is this reform too little? The power of agenda control is actually quite potent. Indeed, in any political system, the power to set the agenda is a cherished commodity that is a prime determinant of who wins and who loses in the political process—and of what that process produces by way of policy outcomes. Any reform that re-allocates agenda control is a very big deal.[14]

In our own system, presidents have so far set the policy agenda for Congress only in the sense that Congress has found it easier, by choice, to organize its business that way. The arrangement is mostly informal. It is Congress that holds formal agenda control, grounded in law. Recall, for example, what happened in the 2013 debate over immigration reform. After securing the Senate's support for a comprehensive immigration package, President Obama hit a roadblock in the House. The problem was not a lack of "yes" votes—for he did indeed have majority support in that chamber, just as he did in the Senate. The problem, rather, was his inability to secure a vote at all. Why did this happen? Because he did not control the agenda— the leadership of the House did. As Obama lamented at the time, "It's very simple: The Republican Speaker of the House, John Boehner, refused to call the bill. Had he called the bill, the overwhelming majority of Democrats and a handful of Republicans would have provided a majority in order to get that done."[15]

This sort of thing is not at all unusual. The majority-party leaders in the House and Senate are powerful precisely because they wield control over the agenda. And Congress is powerful in the legislative process relative to the president precisely because it controls the agenda and he does not. What fast track does is transfer formal agenda power from Congress to the president. Under fast track, Obama would have been able to present his immigration package to Congress, the House and the Senate would have been required to vote on it—and it would have passed, because it had majority support in both chambers.

So now the question. Is fast track somehow "too little" as a constitutional reform? It is surely true that fast track is "little" compared to, say, the adoption of a parliamentary system or the complete reconfiguration of Congress. But those sorts of "big" reforms have no chance of being adopted and are essentially irrelevant. What is so impressive about fast track is that it *is* "little"—it is simple, it is familiar, it is low-risk, and it leaves virtually the entire structure of our constitutional system intact—yet it is also remarkably potent in bringing about big changes in the way American government functions. Coherent policies favored by presidents as effective means of addressing national problems, policies that might once have been blocked or eviscerated but that actually have majority support in both houses, can be voted upon democratically and passed into law. That this can happen—at long last—is hugely liberating and consequential, and a giant step toward the kind of effective government this nation so badly needs.

Proposal powers do more than just unleash opportunities to enact new policies, however. They also change the very nature of public debate. With fast track, members of Congress will no longer be able to dictate the terms of legislative deliberation. Rather, they will have to meet the president on the president's ground. And given its tendency to mimic elite rhetoric, the media can be expected to amplify the very kinds of national and longer-term concerns that preoccupy presidents.[16] This is all to the good. Rather than curtailing public deliberations about pressing and complex problems, granting proposal powers to the president will enrich and enliven them.

The effects of this institutional reform may ripple even further outward. Presidential proposal powers may alter the electoral landscape. It is out of concerns about the next election that majority-party leaders table bills that would split their members. By eliminating this prerogative, fast track would do more than just broaden debate: it would dissolve a long-standing source of party branding and incumbency advantage, a change that may alter the very composition of future Congresses. By forcing members to cast uncomfortable votes, presidents, even in defeat, may pave the way for new challengers in congressional elections.

To be sure, fast track will not break every logjam in Congress. It will not deliver everything that the president wants. Sometimes, the divisions between the major parties will simply be too great, and the divide between national and local prerogatives too wide, for a president with this authority to broker solutions to societal problems. But fast-track authority most certainly will jump-start at least some policies, recast our national discussions about pressing problems, and unleash new electoral pressures on members of Congress—and do so, moreover, in ways that address the most serious defects of our constitutional order. Yes, fast track is "little." But it is the mouse that roared.

What are the downsides? All institutional reforms generate concerns about unintended, and unwanted, consequences. This kind of scrutiny is a healthy thing. In the case of fast track, several lines of criticism come to the fore, and we'd do well to consider them.

Some might worry that fast track would somehow make it too difficult for Congress to represent state and local interests. But as we have already noted, fast track would still allow members of Congress to debate and adopt bills entirely of their own making, just as they do now. The difference is that the pursuit and protection of parochial concerns would no longer be a full-time occupation. Members of Congress would have to pause, periodically, and deliberate on the merits of policies crafted by the president—and do so on the president's terms, which are very much shaped by the drive to seek durable solutions to national problems. Localism would still find expression. But the national interest would have much greater weight in the decision process than it does under the current system, which is *too* localistic. The result is simply a better balance, one that is better for the nation as a whole.

A second potential concern is that, by reducing gridlock and opening new opportunities for coherent governmental action, fast track threatens to give rise to policy instability. This concern also is off the mark. A fundamental flaw built into the current system, after all, is that it is way *too* stable, and stacked against policy changes that are much needed. Separation of powers so profoundly favors the status quo—and the blocking power of special interests—that the government either cannot act or, when it does, is incapable of doing anything that actually resolves major national problems. That a reformed system, due to fast track, would have the capacity to take effective action does not mean that it would somehow be unstable, but rather that it would simply be better able to overcome this massive status quo bias and adopt coherent policies. Yes, there would be more change. But relative to the existing baseline, this is precisely what the nation needs.

For any new policy to be adopted under fast track, moreover, Congress must still give its consent—which means that there must be majority support in the House *and* Senate. A high democratic bar, therefore, must still be surmounted if major policy change is to occur; and that being so, there is no real danger of policy volatility. Far from promoting instability, fast track simply makes it more likely that well-supported policies will get passed—rather than blocked or eviscerated or distorted or weakened—and that the policies that do pass will be more coherent, more effective, and more responsive to national interests.

A third concern that critics are likely to raise about fast track is that it promotes "big government." The underlying notion here is that, if government finds it easier to take action, then government will naturally grow on its own accord. But that needn't be the case at all. The effectiveness of government and the size of government are two different things. The American people can decide for themselves whether they want their government to address a particular problem, and depending on what leaders are in charge, problems may be addressed in varying ways. Leaders and citizens remain perfectly free to choose top-down government programs (which some would call "big government" approaches), programs that rely on markets and the private sector (which some would call "small government" approaches), or something in between. But whatever it does, government should do it effectively. Everyone should want government to be as effective as possible, regardless of what they think about the proper size of government.

Under the current separation-of-powers system, with Congress and all its pathologies at its center, government spends an enormous amount of money paying for policies that don't work very well, can't be fixed or gotten rid of, and stay on the books while more and more programs are layered on over the years—all of which leads to a massive, messy, ineffective governmental system that soaks up the nation's resources without resolving its problems.

Any notion that the current system promotes small government is simply wrong. American government is not small. If its entire corpus is fully measured, including the "submerged state" that people often fail to recognize, it is just as big as most of the welfare states of Europe.[17] Separation of powers has not prevented any of this from happening. The idea that it is a bulwark against big government is a chimera.

Conservatives who favor smaller government—a perfectly legitimate thing to want—should ask themselves: how successful have Republican presidents been at paring back the American welfare state and achieving a smaller, less wasteful government? Answer: despite occupying the White House about 50 percent of the time during the entire postwar era, they have not been successful at all. Why? At least part of the answer is that the policy process is stacked against major policy change—and on those occasions when Republican presidents, particularly Ronald Reagan, sought to make government smaller, they ran headlong into congressional opposition and didn't achieve much. The status quo prevailed. If conservatives want to make government smaller, they need a political system whose decision model gives presidents—including conservative presidents—the capacity for taking effective action. Without fast track or something like it, conservatives will never be able to enact the coherent policy reforms they think are needed. They will be stuck with a big, ineffective government. And the irony is that the separation-of-powers system they hold in such reverence is a prime reason they will be stuck with it.

A fourth and final concern that critics are likely to raise is that fast track threatens to make presidents too powerful. The fact of the matter is that, despite the growth of presidential power since the Progressive years, and despite the dominance of presidents in war and related national security issues, presidents are manifestly underpowered in dealing with the vast range of domestic social problems that face the nation. Constrained at every turn by separation of powers and a fractious Congress, they are incapable of fashioning coherent policy solutions on matters of pressing domestic concern. To be sure, fears about an imperial presidency are legitimate and important for the nation to debate. These fears almost always arise, however, from presidential actions in national security. When it comes to domestic affairs, criticisms of a too-powerful presidency invariably turn on partisanship and depend on whose ox is being gored. Both Republicans and Democrats love presidential power—including unilateral exercises of that power through executive orders—when one of their own is in office, but they hate it when someone from the opposite party holds office. None of this partisan sniping has much to do with an impartial assessment of whether a more powerful president—*regardless of party*—would be good for the nation.

Fast track is not about advantaging one party over another. It doesn't inherently favor the Republicans; it doesn't inherently favor the Democrats. What it does do is recognize reality: this nation has a governmental system that doesn't work, and a key reason it doesn't work is that Congress stands at its center and holds agenda power over public policy. Fast track simply puts that agenda power in the hands of presidents. This reform does *not* somehow make presidents all-powerful. None of the policies they propose can become law unless Congress gives its consent. It simply gives presidents the authority to craft coherent policies, enhances the likelihood that those policies will be democratically adopted, and provides the United States with a more effective form of government.

Looking back over all these potential concerns, then, we find that they are certainly legitimate considerations that deserve to be addressed and discussed, but that there really isn't any significant downside to putting fast track into operation. As a fundamental reform of the American system of government, it is remarkably conservative—keeping almost the entirety of the traditional system in place, but introducing small changes that promise to have big, positive consequences for effective government.

Can this reform get adopted? Although Congress has sometimes given presidents fast-track authority in matters of international trade, the kind of reform we are proposing here cannot be up to Congress to give—and revoke—at will. Fast track needs to be permanently granted to presidents on all policy matters, and this can only be secured through a constitutional amendment that makes it part of the formal structure of American government. Given the high hurdles involved in changing the Constitution, coupled with the polarization that infects contemporary politics, attempts to make this reform a reality are destined to be difficult. But institutional reform is always hard. That doesn't mean, though, that the battle can't be won.

Part of the problem, of course, is that the usual route for amendment is through a two-thirds vote of both houses of Congress—and Congress, needless to say, may not be thrilled at the prospect of shifting its agenda powers to presidents. Yet congressional support, at some moment in time, is still possible. Congress has a long history of delegating tremendous discretion to presidents, in no small part because it recognizes its own weaknesses and comparative disadvantages. With the 1921 Budget and Accounting Act, for example, Congress actively gave presidents the responsibility to propose comprehensive federal budgets, and the role of the Office of Management and Budget has only expanded since then. Throughout the twentieth century, Congress enacted hundreds of bills that ceded extraordinary authority to presidents over the national agenda during times of emergency. On various policy matters—international trade (with fast track), the closing of military bases, the financial integrity of Social Security—Congress has sought out novel decision models (not always successfully) that circumvent its usual processes. And it was Congress—as part of the Gingrich-led Republican revolution in the late 1990s, seeking lower levels of government spending—that adopted the line-item veto, which put substantial new decision power in the hands of presidents (and was later ruled unconstitutional by the Supreme Court).[18]

So we can't rule out the possibility that Congress could come to support a fast-track amendment to the Constitution. The other route to amendment, however, is probably the more promising one. If two-thirds of the states petition Congress for a constitutional convention, Congress has no choice but to call one—and a fast-track amendment could be passed by such a convention, and subsequently ratified by the states, without Congress going along.

The thing that makes either of these options (especially the latter) much more likely is that today's political climate is ripe for institutional reform. The American public is nothing short of disgusted with the federal government. Whereas upwards of 70 percent of Americans during the Eisenhower, Kennedy, and Johnson presidencies professed trust in the federal government, today less that one in four do so. Overall, 30 percent of Americans claim to be "angry" with the federal government and another 55 percent are "frustrated," while just 12 percent are "basically content." The public tends to hold the federal government in much lower regard than state or local governments. And Congress, in particular, is singled out for special opprobrium. Whereas two in three Americans in 1985 claimed to be satisfied with Congress's job performance, less than one in four are today.[19]

These dissatisfactions can only be deepened, and the anger with "politics as usual" intensified, by the ever-growing seriousness of the nation's problems—and the government's manifest inability to deal with them. Escalating debt, millions of undocumented workers laboring in legal limbo, rising temperatures, and economic insecurities are not hypothetical threats looming on a distant horizon. They stand immediately before us, and they lend real urgency to the challenge of governmental reform. To be sure, most citizens pay little attention to politics, and less still to the institutions that govern their lives. But when the gap between society's problems and what the government can actually do to address them becomes sufficiently pronounced and threatening, the need for major institutional change can become a salient public issue—and a driver of politics.

This is exactly what happened more than a hundred years ago, when the dramatic socioeconomic disruptions generated by industrialization gave rise to massive new problems that an outdated government was entirely ill-equipped to handle. The Progressive movement—a "good government" movement, the most powerful in the nation's history—emerged to do something about that. Backed by considerable public support, its leaders achieved great success in attacking the party machines, the corruption, and the abject incompetence of the government they inherited from the past, and they gave the nation a more professional, presidentially led government that was better equipped to address the problems of modern society.

Yet it wasn't enough. The fundamentals—an outdated Constitution, with separation of powers and a parochial Congress at its core—remained firmly in place, ensuring that even this newly reformed government would be out of sync with its dynamic, problem-filled society from the get-go, incapable of taking truly effective action. And over the last century that gap has grown ever bigger as the modern world has continued to change at a frenzied pace—and American government has failed to change with it.

What the nation needs is a second Progressive movement. A movement for modern times.

Taking Responsibility for Our Age

Among Progressive reformers, Herbert Croly singled out Theodore Roosevelt for hearty praise, admiring the energy and innovation he brought to the presidency. Croly's great frustration with the nineteenth-century political ethos was its conviction that, with each generation, the nation's welfare would naturally improve—and the "national promise" would be fulfilled—through continued reliance on an unfettered economy and the founders' revered system of government.[20] Such follies, to Croly's mind, were responsible for the great ills befalling the nation. To deliver on the nation's promise of a better life, each generation must squarely face the problems before it and not shy away from disrupting the institutions inherited from the past. It was this feature of Roosevelt's politics, his commitment to bold reform, that Croly admired most. Roosevelt bravely upheld the proposition that the nation's great challenge was to unshackle itself from the past, to take account of its own problems in its own times, and to fashion its own institutions appropriate and effective for those times.

Roosevelt left his mark on the modern presidency. But were Croly here today, his frustrations would remain. Americans continue to invest faith in the everlasting bounty of the founders' original constitutional order and, indeed, continue to worship the founders themselves—who are treated not merely as wise men but as secular deities. As a nation, we don't just study their accomplishments. We revere them as individuals. We erect monuments to their glory. We make pilgrimages to their places of birth and residence. We devour accounts of their lives in books and on television.[21]

With founder worship so pervasive in American culture, the path to political salvation never involves an updating of the Constitution. On the contrary, the founders' original principles and design are seen as the root source of American democracy and the foundation of what makes this country great. So when we confront new challenges, we should try to intuit how the founders would respond. What would Madison do? Or Jefferson? If these questions can be answered, it is supposed, we'll know how we should proceed in modern times.[22]

When he announced his bid for the Republican presidential nomination in the spring of 2015, Senator Ted Cruz tapped into precisely these kinds of sentiments. After six years of the Obama administration, Cruz intoned, "it is time for truth. It is time for liberty. It is a time to reclaim the Constitution of the United States." Progress, for Cruz, came in the form of reclamation. To rectify the ills of our country, we must "get back to the principles that have made this country great. We will get back and restore that shining city on a hill that is the United States of America."[23]

These themes are not exclusive to the ideological right. Democrats and Republicans alike cloak themselves in the mantle of constitutional fidelity, which functions as a rhetorical trump card.

In the language of American politics, the Constitution is treated as something of a sacred document that—much like the Bible—is beyond reproach as the written embodiment of wisdom, truth, and justice. People may differ, perhaps vehemently, about what the Constitution means and what the three branches of government are properly allowed to do; the Constitution is open to interpretation, just as the Bible is. But that the Constitution is fundamentally good, and that Americans are uncommonly fortunate to have it as the guiding law of the land, is almost never questioned. To question it is to commit some sort of heresy.

Yet that shouldn't be so. Questioning the Constitution should be a normal and valued part of our political culture as a nation. The Constitution affects our lives in profound ways, and if it gives us a government that can't meet the needs of our times, then we need to simply recognize as much—honestly, openly, objectively— and do something about it. Thomas Jefferson, in fact, was very clear about exactly that. Writing almost thirty years after the Constitution was adopted, here is what he had to say:

> Some men look at constitutions with sanctimonious reverence, and deem them like the arc of the covenant, too sacred to be touched. They ascribe to the men of the preceding age a wisdom more than human, and suppose what they did to be beyond amendment. . . . [But] laws and institutions must go hand in hand with the progress of the human mind. As that becomes more developed, more enlightened, as new discoveries are made, new truths disclosed, and manners and opinions change with the change of circumstances, institutions must advance also, and keep pace with the times. We might as well require a man to wear still the coat which fitted him when a

boy, as civilized society to remain ever under the regimen of their barbarous ancestors.[24]

As modern citizens, should we be asking, "What would Jefferson do?" This is precisely the question Jefferson himself thought we should *not* be asking. He and his contemporaries designed a government for their times, not for a future society whose transformations and challenges they could not foresee. It would be up to future generations to bring government and society into sync as times changed. As historian H. W. Brands has well observed, "The Founders got the country off to a good start, but they would have been the first to admit that it was no more than a start. They were acutely aware of the continuing nature of their experiment in self-government, and they expected future generations to accomplish as much as they had. They would have dismissed as ludicrous the notion that theirs was a blessed generation, to which others might never compare."[25]

If we Americans can internalize this basic point, we can embrace a much healthier view of our admirable but outdated Constitution—and refuse to be prisoners of the past. The United States of today is profoundly different from the United States of 1789, and it is up to us to fashion political institutions that allow for effective government in *our* times. The founders cannot save us. We must save ourselves.

Acknowledgments

For nearly a decade, the two of us have worked together closely in developing the ideas presented here about the constitutional origins of ineffective government, the pathologies of Congress, and the promise of a stronger presidency. From start to finish, this book was a seamless collaboration, and on every page the mark of each author's influence can be found. Because one name needs to go first on the title page and the other name second, we have chosen to simply order them alphabetically. That is the convention in political science (and most other areas of social science) when the authors' contributions are equally important, so we follow it here.

While we were writing this book, and indeed much earlier, while we were first hashing out our ideas and doing background research, we both benefitted from the support, expertise, and enthusiasm of an amazing team of research assistants. At the University of Chicago, Ethan Porter researched and drafted early versions of some of the case studies that appear in Chapter 4, and Susan Mallaney was the ultimate utility player, helping out with research, tracking down citations, editing prose, and much more. At Stanford University, Patrick Kennedy carried out extensive research very early on across a number of policy realms, offered creative ideas, and was pivotal in getting this project out of the starting gate. Lily Lamboy covered a vast substantive terrain, contributing research on the founders and on numerous and diverse realms of public policy that were crucial to the arguments of Chapters 2 and 3. Verlan Lewis provided key assistance with references and fact-checking as the final document took shape and offered insights that helped firm up our analysis. At both universities, meanwhile, students in classes we have taught on political institutions and the American presidency have shaped our thinking about why our government does such a poor job of solving societal problems and what might be done about it.

We have benefitted from discussions over the years with colleagues too numerous to mention at the University of Chicago, Stanford, and other universities, and we want them to know that we value their input and inspiration. We want to give special thanks to Betsy Palay, who read the entire manuscript and gave us extraordinarily insightful suggestions for improvement. We also want to thank Jack Rakove for his very useful comments on an early version of Chapter 1.

Lastly, we have had the great fortune to work with first-class editors at Basic Books, Dan Gerstle and Ben Platt, whose experience, perspective, and guidance helped immensely in the crafting of this book.

Notes

Introduction

1. See, e.g., Thomas Mann and Norman Ornstein, *It's Even Worse Than It Looks: How the American Constitutional System Collided with the New Politics of Extremism* (New York, NY: Basic Books, 2012); Marc J. Hetherington and Thomas J. Rudolph, *Why Washington Won't Work: Polarization, Political Trust, and the Governing Crisis* (Chicago, IL: University of Chicago Press, 2015); Barbara Sinclair, *Party Wars: Polarization and the Politics of National Policy Making* (Norman, OK: University of Oklahoma Press, 2006); Mike Lofgren, *The Party Is Over: How Republicans Went Crazy, Democrats Became Useless, and the Middle Class Got Shafted* (New York, NY: Penguin Books, 2013).

2. An impressive body of scholarly literature, marshaled by social scientists in hundreds of studies over a period of many decades, documents the ineffectiveness of policies produced by our national government. Almost thirty years ago, Peter Rossi, a respected sociologist with long experience in policy evaluation, offered an overview of the scholarly research on the subject at the time and concluded that "few impact assessments of large scale social programs have found that the programs in question had any net impact," adding that "the better designed the impact assessment of a social program, the more likely is the resulting estimate of net impact to be zero" ("The Iron Law of Evaluation and Other Metallic Rules," in *Research in Social Problems and Public Policy,* vol. 4, ed. Joann Miller and Michael Lewis (Greenwich, CT: Jai Press, 1987), 3–20). Since then there have been

many more studies, and the studies have been more sophisticated—but their downbeat findings have been much the same. Especially instructive overviews and insightful perspectives on this body of work include: Peter Schuck, *Why Government Fails So Often: And How It Can Do Better* (Princeton, NJ: Princeton University Press, 2014); Clifford Winston, *Government Failure Versus Market Failure: Microeconomic Policy Research and Government Performance* (Washington, DC: Brookings Institution Press and American Enterprise Institute for Public Policy Research, 2006); Derek Bok, *The Trouble with Government* (Cambridge, MA: Harvard University Press, 2001); Jonathan Rauch, *Government's End: Why Washington Stopped Working* (Washington, DC: PublicAffairs, 1999).

Peter Schuck's assessment of the available social science in *Why Government Fails So Often*, which is thoughtful and encyclopedic and surely the most comprehensive to date, leads him to the following summary of the evidence:

> The pages of this book are littered with scores of federal policy failures—programs that create fewer benefits than costs, are cost-ineffective, or are perversely targeted—and only a handful of major successes. . . .
>
> Unfortunately, this dismal record is not confined to a limited policy space or only a few policy instruments. To the contrary, the failed programs discussed in this book cover a vast range of domestic policies, as well as all of the specific policy tools . . . grants, contracts, insurance, subsidies, regulation, and the rest. Nor are these failures marginal or insignificant. In fact, they include some of our largest, most durable, most visible, and most fiercely defended programs. Together, they account for a substantial share of total non-defense discretionary spending. (p. 371)

We are not just throwing stones, then, in saying that American government is ineffective. A large body of social science evidence confirms as much. Our purpose here is to move beyond all this evidence, to build upon it by showing that there are good reasons for *expecting* government to be ineffective, and to chart a productive way forward in order to do something about it.

3. As we will discuss in Chapter 2, members of Congress are not exclusively parochial in their approaches to policy, and national concerns and political forces are not unimportant to them. Our point, here and throughout the book, is simply that members are strongly influenced by the parochial pulls of their states and districts—and that in the mix of factors that may shape their behavior, these localistic, electorally driven concerns are particularly consequential.

4. We are not the first to argue that the Constitution is unsuited to modern times. The best known of these critiques—by legal scholar Sanford Levinson and political scientist Robert Dahl, among others—argue that the Constitution fails to reflect modern democratic values. (See: Sanford Levinson, *Our Undemocratic Constitution: Where the Constitution Goes Wrong* (New York, NY: Oxford University Press, 2008); Robert Dahl, *How Democratic Is the American Constitution?*, 2nd ed. (New Haven, CT: Yale University Press, 2003)). And they are right. It creates a Senate, for example, in which Wyoming has just as much voting power as California, and it requires that presidents be chosen by an archaic, nonsensical Electoral College rather than by direct popular vote. We could go on. But as much as we agree with these arguments, we will not pursue them here because our focus is squarely on the Constitution's perverse consequences for effective government—a line of constitutional analysis that has largely been off the radar screens of those who study American government. There was a short burst of intellectual activity on this subject during the 1980s, led by the Brookings Institution's James Sundquist and former presidential counsel Lloyd Cutler, but their reformist arguments attracted little lasting attention. (See: James Sundquist, *Constitutional Reform and Effective Government* (Washington, DC: Brookings Institution Press, 1992); Lloyd N. Cutler, "Now Is the Time for All Good Men," *William and Mary Law Review* 30, no. 2 (1989): 387–402.)

5. We are not arguing, needless to say, that the Constitution is the only source of ineffective government, but rather that it is the most fundamental source, and thus that it is of pervasive importance. For an extensive treatment of many other (but often related) sources of ineffectiveness in American government—problems, for example, of information, incentives, and fractured organization—see Schuck, *Why Government Fails So Often*. Also, we should emphasize that, while our focus in this book is on the constitutional foundations of ineffective government, we aren't claiming that Congress has never succeeded in taking effective legislative action, for there are surely cases when it has—the Voting Rights Act, the Morrill Act, and airline deregulation are examples. But these cases are exceptions, and our aim here is to explain why the central tendency of the American governmental system is toward ineffective policy. For a discussion of Congress's rare successes—with the emphasis (quite properly) on "rare"—see again Schuck, *Why Government Fails So Often*.

6. See, e.g., H. W. Brands, "Founders Chic: Our Reverence for the Fathers Has Got Out of Hand," *Atlantic Monthly,* September 2003, 108; Jeremy D.

Bailey, *James Madison and Constitutional Imperfection* (New York, NY: Cambridge University Press, 2015).

7. See, e.g., "Beyond Distrust: How Americans View Their Government," Pew Research Center, November 23, 2015, http://www.people-press.org/2015 /11/23/beyond-distrust-how-americans-view-their-government/; "Presidential Approval," Pew Research Center, July 20, 2015, http://www.pewresearch.org /data-trend/political-attitudes/presidential-approval/; Jeffrey M. Jones, "Congress' Job Approval Rating Slips to 11%," *Gallup*, November 11, 2015, http:// www.gallup.com/poll/186581/congress-job-approval-rating-slips.aspx.

8. Under such a system, the executive arises out of the majority party (or coalition) in the legislature. The executive is then able to take the lead in crafting policies to address the nation's pressing problems, knowing that those policies will have majority support in—and be adopted by—the legislature.

9. Our book is not the only contemporary argument on behalf of a stronger American presidency, but it highlights a very different set of problems, just as it proceeds according to a very different logic, than previous scholarship. Whereas other works tend to focus on security issues and various kinds of international policy challenges (see, e.g., Eric Posner and Adrian Vermeule, *Terror in the Balance: Security, Liberty, and the Courts* (New York, NY: Oxford University Press, 2006); John Yoo, *The Powers of War and Peace: The Constitution and Foreign Affairs After 9/11* (Chicago, IL: University of Chicago Press, 2008)), ours is primarily concerned with the government's inability to solve domestic policy problems. And whereas much of this other work tries, in one way or another, to make the case for a stronger presidency on the grounds that it accords with a particular reading of the Constitution, (e.g., Steven Calebresi and Christopher Yoo, *The Unitary Executive: Presidential Power from Washington to Bush* (New Haven, CT: Yale University Press, 2012)), ours sees constitutional failings—or, more exactly, the fact that our Constitution is out of sync with modern times—as the impetus for institutional change. In spirit, our book is closest to Eric Posner and Adrian Vermeule's *The Executive Unbound: After the Madisonian Republic* (New York, NY: Oxford University Press, 2011). (For a particularly thoughtful review essay on this book, see Richard Pildes, "Law and the President," *Harvard Law Review*, vol. 125, 1381–1424). Our line of argumentation, the evidence we cull, and the specific reforms we endorse, however, differ in important respects from Posner and Vermeule's book.

10. In the lexicon of today's politics, *progressive* has become another label for *liberal* and thus is associated with the pursuit of big government, high taxes, and all the rest. This is unfortunate and, as a matter of history, misleading. As we will discuss in more detail in Chapter 1, it is true that the Progressives of one hundred years ago wanted government to be bigger than it was by taking a positive role in addressing some of the ravages and disruptions of an industrializing society. But at that time, government was doing very little. The Progressives simply wanted a government equipped to take action against emerging problems—such as price-fixing, child labor, and tainted meat—that were so basic and so egregious that in today's world everyone, liberals and conservatives alike, would regard addressing them as proper governmental responsibilities. None of this has anything to do with what critics now refer to as "big government." The leaders of the Progressive movement, it should be added, came from both political parties. Theodore Roosevelt and Robert LaFollette, for example, were Republicans. Woodrow Wilson was a Democrat. See, e.g., Robert H. Wiebe, *The Search for Order, 1877–1920* (New York, NY: Hill and Wang, 1967); Michael McGerr, *A Fierce Discontent: The Rise and Fall of the Progressive Movement in America* (New York, NY: Oxford University Press, 2003); Sidney Milkis, *Theodore Roosevelt, the Progressive Party, and the Transformation of American Democracy* (Lawrence, KS: University Press of Kansas, 2009).

Chapter 1: The Constitution, Social Change, and the Progressives

1. Historians sometimes refer to the men who participated in the Constitutional Convention and actually wrote the Constitution as the *framers* and use the term *founders* to refer to the larger group of people who, from the time of the Revolutionary War, were key players in the creation of the United States as a nation. By these definitions, our own analysis is mainly concerned with the framers, but not always. Jefferson, for example, was technically not a framer because he was serving as ambassador to France at the time of the Constitutional Convention and was not physically present (although he was in communication with Madison). To avoid ambiguities and awkwardness in language, we find it helpful to simply use the term *founders* for the key players who were influential around the time the Constitution was written, and we will adopt this convention throughout the book.

2. For an account of the universal appeal of the principles of the American Revolution, see Danielle Allen, *Our Declaration: A Reading of the Declaration of Independence in Defense of Equality* (New York, NY: Liveright Publishing Corporation, 2014). For an account of the democratic character of the American founding, see Bernard Bailyn, *The Ideological Origins of the American Revolution* (Cambridge, MA: Harvard University Press, 1967); Gordon Wood, *The Creation of the American Republic* (Chapel Hill, NC: University of North Carolina Press, 1969); Gordon Wood, *The Radicalism of the American Revolution* (New York, NY: Alfred A. Knopf, 1992).

3. Strictly speaking, the founders created a republican form of government, not a pure democracy. And the reasons why they did so relate, in no small part, to their distrust of average citizens, which we discuss at greater length below. It is incontrovertible, though, that the founders created a government that was a good deal more democratic than the one they had known, at least for white, male property owners. We discuss this at greater length below.

4. James Madison, "The Federalist, 10," in *The Federalist Papers,* ed. Lawrence Goldman (Oxford, UK: Oxford University Press, 2008), 54–55.

5. Richard Hofstadter, *The American Political Tradition: And the Men Who Made It* (New York, NY: Alfred A. Knopf, 1948; Vintage Books, 1989), 9. Citations refer to the Vintage Books edition. For an overview of the undemocratic elements of the Constitution, see also Robert Dahl, *How Democratic Is the Constitution?* (New Haven, CT: Yale University Press, 2001).

6. For an account of how white male suffrage was expanded in the early nineteenth century, see Sean Wilentz, *The Rise of American Democracy: Jefferson to Lincoln* (New York, NY: W. W. Norton & Company, 2005).

7. Judith Apter Klinghoffer and Lois Elkis, "'The Petticoat Electors': Women's Suffrage in New Jersey, 1776–1807," *Journal of the Early Republic* 12, no. 2 (1992): 159–193.

8. The three-fifths rule was actually adopted as a political compromise between the northern and southern states for determining how much representation the South would have in the new House. The southern states wanted each slave to be counted as one person for the purpose of determining a state's population and thus its number of representatives in the House. The northern states didn't want slaves to be counted at all, giving the North a greater representational edge over the South. The compromise was that each slave would be counted as three-fifths of a person—which gave the South additional repre-

sentation and voting power in the House (but also required that southern states pay additional federal taxes).

9. For historical perspective on slavery and the founders (including early presidents), see Paul Finkelman, *Slavery and the Founders: Race and Liberty in the Age of Jefferson,* 3rd ed. (New York, NY: Routledge, 2014); James Oliver Horton and Lois E. Horton, *Slavery and the Making of America* (New York, NY: Oxford University Press, 2004).

10. For a description of modern Americans' lack of knowledge of slavery at the time of the American founding, see James Oliver Horton, "Slavery in American History: An Uncomfortable National Dialogue," in *Slavery and Public History: The Tough Stuff of American History,* ed. James Oliver Horton and Lois E. Horton (New York, NY: Free Press, 2006), 35–56.

11. Alexander Hamilton, "The Federalist, 1," in *The Federalist Papers,* ed. Lawrence Goldman (Oxford, UK: Oxford University Press, 2008), 11.

12. See Sidney M. Milkis and Michael Nelson, *The American Presidency: Origins and Developments, 1776–2011* (Washington, DC: Congressional Quarterly Press, 2012).

13. James Madison, "The Federalist, 48," in *The Federalist Papers,* ed. Lawrence Goldman (Oxford, UK: Oxford University Press, 2008), 246.

14. Madison, "The Federalist, 10," 50.

15. Madison, "The Federalist, 51," 257.

16. Richard Neustadt, *Presidential Power and the Modern Presidents: The Politics of Leadership from Roosevelt to Reagan* (New York, NY: John Wiley & Sons, 1960; The Free Press, 1991), 29. Citations refer to the Free Press edition.

17. Charles de Secondat, Baron de Montesquieu, *The Spirit of the Laws* (New York, NY: Cambridge University Press, [1748] 1989).

18. John Adams, *The Works of John Adams, Second President of the United States: With a Life of the Author, Notes and Illustrations, by his Grandson Charles Francis Adams,* vol. 6 (Boston: Little, Brown and Company, 1851), 63.

19. John Jay, "The Federalist, 64," in *The Federalist Papers,* ed. Lawrence Goldman (Oxford, UK: Oxford University Press, 2008), 318; Alexander Hamilton, "The Federalist, 70," in *The Federalist Papers,* ed. Lawrence Goldman (Oxford, UK: Oxford University Press, 2008).

20. We want to be clear that, here and throughout the book, we consistently use masculine pronouns when referring to presidents only because, from the time of the founders until today (early 2016), the office of the presidency has

exclusively been occupied by men. This male monopoly is very likely to come to an end sometime in the near future. But until that happens, we think it makes sense to continue using pronouns that reflect the historical reality of the office.

21. For an overview of the founders' theory of presidential selection, see James Ceaser, *Presidential Selection: Theory and Development* (Princeton, NJ: Princeton University Press, 1979).

22. Figures are from Bureau of the Census, US Department of Commerce and Labor, *Heads of Families at the First Census of the United States Taken in the Year 1790: Records of the State Enumerations 1782–1785—Virginia* (Washington, DC: US Government Printing Office, 1908), 8, http://www2 .census.gov/prod2/decennial/documents/1790m-02.pdf. Virginia's population figure includes Kentucky, which was part of Virginia at the time of the Constitutional Convention.

23. For a theoretical perspective on the consequences of veto points for public policy and the status quo, see George Tsebelis, *Veto Players: How Political Institutions Work* (Princeton, NJ: Princeton University Press, 2002).

24. For an account of the emergence of standing committees in the House of Representatives, see Jeffrey Jenkins, "Property Rights and the Emergence of Standing Committee Dominance in the Nineteenth Century," *Legislative Studies Quarterly* 23, no. 4 (1998): 493–519. For historical background on the filibuster, see Sarah A. Binder and Steven S. Smith, *Politics or Principle: Filibustering in the United States Senate* (Washington, DC: Brookings Institution Press, 1996).

25. For accounts of the parochial nature of congressional politics, see David Mayhew, *Congress: The Electoral Connection* (New Haven, CT: Yale University Press, 1974); John A. Ferejohn, *Pork Barrel Politics: Rivers and Harbors Legislation, 1947–1968* (Stanford, CA: Stanford University Press, 1974); Richard Fenno, *Home Style: House Members in their Districts* (Boston, MA: Little, Brown and Company, 1978). Many more references are provided in Chapter 2. As we will discuss in that chapter, national pressures have grown more relevant to members of Congress in recent decades—but even so, these legislators remain strongly influenced by the forces of parochialism.

26. Bureau of the Census, US Department of Commerce and Labor, *Heads of Families at the First Census of the United States Taken in the Year 1790*, 8; "The 1790 Census," US Census Bureau, last revised August 14, 2015, http:// www.census.gov/history/www/through_the_decades/fast_facts/1790_fast _facts.html; "US Population, Land Area and Density, 1790–2000," United

States History, Online Highways, http://www.u-s-history.com/pages/h986 .html; Bureau of the Census, US Department of Commerce, "Table 4. Population: 1790 to 1990," *1990 Census of Population and Housing: Population and Housing Unit Counts,* 1990 CPH-2-1, August 20, 1993, 5, https://www.census .gov/prod/cen1990/cph2/cph-2-1-1.pdf.

27. "The 2010 Census," US Census Bureau, last revised August 14, 2015, http://www.census.gov/history/www/through_the_decades/fast_facts/2010 _fast_facts.html; "2012 Census Highlights," US Department of Agriculture, http://www.agcensus.usda.gov/Publications/2012/Online_Resources/High lights/Farm_Demographics/; J. David Hacker, "Decennial Life Tables for the White Population of the United States, 1790–1900," *Historical Methods* 43, no. 2 (April 2010): 45–79, http://www.ncbi.nlm.nih.gov/pmc/articles/PMC28 85717/; "Life Expectancy at Birth, Male (Years)," The World Bank, http://data .worldbank.org/indicator/SP.DYN.LE00.MA.IN; "Life Expectancy at Birth, Female (Years)," The World Bank, http://data.worldbank.org/indicator/SP.DYN .LE00.FE.IN/countries; "Annual Estimates of the Resident Population for Incorporated Places of 50,000 or More, Ranked by July 1, 2014 Population: April 1, 2010 to July 1, 2014," American FactFinder, US Census Bureau, Population Division, May 2015, http://factfinder2.census.gov/bkmk/table/1.0/en /PEP/2014/PEPANNRSIP.US12A.

28. The GDP figures provided here are taken from data presented in Louis Johnston and Samuel H. Williamson, "What Was the U.S. GDP Then?," MeasuringWorth.com, 2015, http://www.measuringworth.org/usgdp/. The most recent figures are for 2014. The deflator takes 2009 dollars as the base. Nominal data on import and exports for 1790 are taken from Douglass C. North, "The United States Balance of Payments, 1790–1860," in *Trends in the American Economy in the Nineteenth Century,* ed. The Conference on Research in Income and Wealth, National Bureau of Economic Research (Princeton, NJ: Princeton University Press, 1960), 577, http://www.nber.org/chapters/c2491 .pdf. More recent data on nominal imports and exports refer to 2013 and are taken from John G. Murphy, "2013: The Year in Trade," Above the Fold (blog), US Chamber of Commerce, February 6, 2014, https://www.uschamber .com/blog/2013-year-trade. All the import and export data were deflated using the MeasuringWorth 2009 GDP deflator.

29. "A Short History of the Department of State," US Department of State, Office of the Historian, https://history.state.gov/departmenthistory/short-history

/staffing; Spencer C. Tucker, *Almanac of American Military History,* vol. 1 (Denver, CO: ABC-CLIO, 2013), 408; "Mission," US Department of State, http://careers.state.gov/learn/what-we-do/mission; "Armed Forces Strength Figures for August 31, 2015," US Department of Defense, https://www.dmdc .osd.mil/appj/dwp/dwp_reports.jsp.

30. See, e.g., H. W. Brands, "Founders Chic: Our Reverence for the Fathers Has Gotten Out of Hand," *Atlantic Monthly,* September 2003, 108.

31. Samuel Huntington, *Political Order in Changing Societies* (New Haven, CT: Yale University Press, 1965); Francis Fukuyama, *Political Order and Political Decay: From the Industrial Revolution to the Globalization of Democracy* (New York, NY: Farrar, Straus and Giroux, 2014).

32. On how the lack of fit between governing institutions and society can stifle economic growth, see Douglass C. North, *Institutions, Institutional Change and Economic Performance* (Cambridge, UK: Cambridge University Press, 1990); Daron Acemoglu and James A. Robinson, *Why Nations Fail: The Origins of Power, Prosperity, and Poverty* (New York, NY: Crown Publishing, 2012).

33. For an overview of the rapid changes that America underwent shortly after the establishment of the American republic, see Daniel Walker Howe, *What God Hath Wrought: The Transformation of America, 1815–1848* (New York, NY: Oxford University Press, 2007).

34. Zoltan Kovecses, *American English: An Introduction* (Peterborough, ON: Broadview Press, 2000), 19; Bureau of the Census, US Department of Commerce and Labor, *Heads of Families at the First Census of the United States Taken in the Year 1790,* 8; Steven E. Woodworth and Kenneth J. Winkle, *Atlas of the Civil War* (Oxford, UK: Oxford University Press, 2004).

35. Bureau of the Census, US Department of Commerce, *Historical Statistics of the United States, 1789–1945* (Washington, DC: US Government Printing Office, 1949), 16–38; "The 1860 Census," US Census Bureau, last revised August 14, 2015, http://www.census.gov/history/www/through_the_decades /fast_facts/1860_fast_facts.html.

36. John Aldrich, *Why Parties?: A Second Look* (Chicago, IL: University of Chicago Press, 2011), 70–101.

37. Robert V. Remini, *Martin Van Buren and the Making of the Democratic Party* (New York, NY: Columbia University Press, 1959); John Aldrich, *Why Parties?,* 102–129; Michael F. Holt, *The Rise and Fall of the American Whig*

Party: Jacksonian Politics and the Onset of the Civil War (New York, NY: Oxford University Press, 1999).

38. Arthur M. Schlesinger Jr., *The Age of Jackson* (Boston, MA: Little, Brown and Company, 1945); Richard Bensel, *The American Ballot Box in the Mid-Nineteenth Century* (New York, NY: Cambridge University Press, 2004).

39. This isn't to say that the United States wouldn't have prospered even more had the federal government been effective, but rather that, with so much else working in its favor, the nation managed to prosper during the 1800s notwithstanding the burden and drag of an ineffective government.

40. Richard Sutch, "Gross Domestic Product: 1790–2002 [Continuous Annual Series]," Table Ca9-19, in vol. 3, *Historical Statistics of the United States, Earliest Times to the Present: Millennial Edition,* ed. Susan B. Carter et al. (New York, NY: Cambridge University Press, 2006), 26, http://hsus.cambridge .org/HSUSWeb/search/searchTable.do?id=Ca9-19.

41. Bureau of the Census, US Department of Commerce, "Table 4. Population: 1790 to 1990," *1990 Census of Population and Housing: Population and Housing Unit Counts,* 1990 CPH-2-1, August 20, 1993, 5, https://www.census .gov/prod/cen1990/cph2/cph-2-1-1.pdf.

42. Bureau of the Census, *Historical Statistics,* 25–38; "First- and Second-Generation Share of the Population, 1900–2015," Pew Research Center, http://www.pewhispanic.org/2015/09/28/statistical-portrait-of-the-foreign -born-population-in-the-united-states-1960-2013-key-charts/#2013-fb-first -second-gen.

43. Louis P. Cain, "Railroad Mileage and Equipment: 1830–1890," Table Df874-881, in vol. 4, *Historical Statistics of the United States, Earliest Times to the Present: Millennial Edition,* ed. Susan B. Carter et al. (New York, NY: Cambridge University Press, 2006), 916, http://hsus.cambridge.org/HSUSWeb /search/searchTable.do?id=Df882-885; "Retail Mail Order Competition," *Chicago Dry Goods Reporter* 31 (January 5, 1901), 25.

44. On the disruptive social changes taking place during this era, along with the political responses, see Robert H. Wiebe, *The Search for Order, 1877– 1920* (New York, NY: Hill and Wang, 1967); Michael McGerr, *A Fierce Discontent: The Rise and Fall of the Progressive Movement in America* (New York, NY: Oxford University Press, 2003).

45. To avoid confusion, we want to reiterate that the term *Progressives* refers to the participants in this specific movement around the turn of the

twentieth century and not the liberals of today, who are sometimes referred to as *progressives* in the language of modern politics. On the Progressive movement, see Wiebe, *The Search for Order*; McGerr, *A Fierce Discontent*; Jack H. Knott and Gary J. Miller, *Reforming Bureaucracy: The Politics of Institutional Choice* (New York, NY: Pearson Publishing, 1987); Sidney Milkis, *Theodore Roosevelt, the Progressive Party, and the Transformation of American Democracy* (Lawrence, KS: University Press of Kansas, 2009); Michael McGerr, *A Fierce Discontent: The Rise and Fall of the Progressive Movement in America* (New York, NY: Oxford University Press, 2003).

46. Herbert Croly, *The Promise of the American Life* (New Brunswick, NJ: Transaction Publishers, [1909] 1993), 270.

47. Woodrow Wilson, *Congressional Government: A Study in American Politics*, 15th ed. (Boston, MA: Houghton Mifflin Company, [1885] 1913), 102.

48. Woodrow Wilson, *The New Freedom: A Call for the Emancipation of the Generous Energies of a People* (New York, NY: Doubleday, Page & Company, 1918), 3–4, 19–20.

49. For a discussion of how the primary system has diminished the role of party organizations, see, e.g., Ceaser, *Presidential Selection*. For a historical account of how the rise of executive-centered national administration diminished the power of state and local parties, see, e.g., Sidney Milkis, *The President and the Parties: The Transformation of the American Party System Since the New Deal* (New York, NY: Oxford University Press, 1993).

50. For a fuller account of how this happened, see Stephen Skowronek, *Building a New American State: The Expansion of National Administrative Capacities, 1877–1920* (New York, NY: Cambridge University Press, 1982). For a brief summary of the importance of the national state in American politics, see Daniel Carpenter, "The Evolution of National Bureaucracy in the United States," in *The Executive Branch,* ed. Joel D. Aberbach and Mark A. Peterson (New York, NY: Oxford University Press 2005), 41–71.

51. Reflecting on the period, the political scientist Peri Arnold writes, "Beset by the changing economy, corrupted local governments, a maldistribution of wealth in the face of growing poverty, overwhelming waves of immigrants, and the threatening urban environment, middle-class Americans saw government as necessary for solving social and economic problems. In contrast to the parochial Congress, it was the presidency that presented a possibility for leadership to address what middle-class Americans identified as the public inter-

est." (*Remaking the Presidency: Roosevelt, Taft, and Wilson, 1901–1916* (Lawrence, KS: University Press of Kansas, 2009), 12–13).

52. Henry Jones Ford, *The Rise and Growth of American Politics: A Sketch of Constitutional Development* (New York, NY: MacMillan, 1898), 194, 250, 283.

53. For a description of how TR and Wilson helped transform the presidency through the use of public rhetoric, see Jeffrey Tulis, *The Rhetorical Presidency* (Princeton, NJ: Princeton University Press, 1997).

54. For an overview of TR's political thought and an analysis of how his political thought and actions departed from previous norms, see Jean Yarbrough, *Theodore Roosevelt and the American Political Tradition* (Lawrence, KS: University Press of Kansas, 2012). Theodore Roosevelt, *The Autobiography of Theodore Roosevelt* (New York, NY: Macmillan, 1913), 198.

55. This distinction between the modern and premodern presidency was famously made by Neustadt in *Presidential Power and the Modern Presidents*. See also Woodrow Wilson, *Constitutional Government in the United States* (New York, NY: Columbia University Press, 1908).

56. Milkis, *Theodore Roosevelt, the Progressive Party, and the Transformation of American Democracy*.

57. Skowronek, *Building a New American State*.

58. For an overview of how expectations for the presidency changed in the twentieth century, see Theodore Lowi, *The Personal President: Power Invested, Promise Unfulfilled* (Ithaca, NY: Cornell University Press, 1985).

Chapter 2: Congress and the Pathologies of American Government

1. For a calculation of the high legislative productivity of this period, see David Mayhew, *Divided We Govern* (New Haven, CT: Yale University Press, 2002).

2. For an account of the legislative politics of these Johnson years, see Julian E. Zelizer, *The Fierce Urgency of Now: Lyndon Johnson, Congress, and the Battle for the Great Society* (New York, NY: Penguin Press, 2015).

3. The account to follow is based on material presented in R. Douglas Arnold, *Congress and the Bureaucracy: A Theory of Influence* (New Haven, CT: Yale University Press, 1979).

4. Arnold, *Congress and the Bureaucracy*, 168.

5. On interest groups and their activities in Congress, see Allan J. Cigler, Burdett A. Loomis, and Anthony J. Nownes, eds., *Interest Group Politics* (Washington, DC: Congressional Quarterly Press, 2015); Lee Drutman, *The Business of America Is Lobbying: How Corporations Became Politicized and Politics Became More Corporate* (New York, NY: Oxford University Press, 2015); Jon R. Wright, *Interest Groups and Congress: Lobbying, Contributions, and Influence* (New York, NY: Pearson Publishing, 2002); Jonathan Rauch, *Government's End: Why Washington Stopped Working* (New York, NY: Public Affairs, 1999). The most notable recent Supreme Court case to dismantle campaign finance restrictions is *Citizens United v. Federal Election Commission*, 588 U.S. 310 (2010). On the reelection incentive and parochialism, see, e.g., David R. Mayhew, *Congress: The Electoral Connection* (New Haven, CT: Yale University Press, 1974); Morris P. Fiorina, *Representatives, Roll Calls, and Constituency* (Lexington, MA: Lexington Books, 1974); Richard F. Fenno, *Home Style: House Members in Their Districts* (Upper Saddle River, NJ: Pearson, 1978); John W. Kingdon, *Congressmen's Voting Decisions*, 3rd ed. (Ann Arbor, MI: University of Michigan Press, 1989); Barry R. Weingast and William J. Marshall, "The Industrial Organization of Congress; Or, Why Legislators, Like Firms, Are Not Organized as Markets," *Journal of Political Economy* 96, no. 1 (February 1988): 132–163; R. Douglas Arnold, *The Logic of Congressional Action* (New Haven, CT: Yale University Press, 1990); Robert M. Stein and Kenneth N. Bickers, *Perpetuating the Pork Barrel: Policy Subsystems and American Democracy* (New York, NY: Cambridge University Press, 1997); Jonathan Rauch, *Government's End*; Benjamin J. Bishin, "Constituency Influence in Congress: Does Subconstituency Matter?" *Legislative Studies Quarterly* 25, no. 3 (2000): 389–415; Brandice Canes-Wrone, David W. Brady, and John F. Cogan, "Out of Step, Out of Office: Electoral Accountability and House Members' Voting," *American Political Science Review* 96, no. 1 (2002): 127–140; Diana Evans, *Greasing the Wheels: Using Pork Barrel Projects to Build Majority Coalitions in Congress* (New York, NY: Cambridge University Press, 2004); Kristina C. Miller, *Constituency Representation in Congress: The View from Capitol Hill* (New York, NY: Cambridge University Press, 2015); Rebecca Thorpe, *The American Warfare State: The Domestic Politics of Military Spending* (Chicago, IL: University of Chicago Press, 2014).

6. A large and long-standing research tradition in political science also examines the nationalization of congressional elections. For examinations of specific nationalizing forces in congressional elections, see Michael Lewis-Beck and Mary Stegmaier, "Economic Determinants of Electoral Outcomes," *Annual Review of Political Science* 3 (2000): 183–219; James Campbell and Joe Sumners, "Presidential Coattails in Senate Elections," *American Political Science Review* 84, no. 2 (1990): 513–524; B. K. Song, "The Effect of Television on Electoral Politics" (working paper, Harvard University, 2014). For a general discussion of the topic, see Barry C. Burden and Amber Wichowsky, "Local and National Forces in Congressional Elections," in *The Oxford Handbook of American Elections and Political Behavior,* ed. Jan E. Leighley (New York, NY: Oxford University Press, 2010), 453–470; David Brady, Robert D'Onofrio, and Morris Fiorina, "The Nationalization of Electoral Forces Revisited," in *Change and Continuity in House Elections,* ed. David Brady and John Cogan (Stanford, CA: Stanford University Press, 2000), 130–148. For an older but highly influential literature on the nationalizing effects of "realigning elections," see Walter Dean Burnham, *Critical Elections and the Mainsprings of American Politics* (New York, NY: W. W. Norton & Company, 1971); David Brady, *Critical Elections and Congressional Policy Making* (Stanford, CA: Stanford University Press, 1988); James Sundquist, *Dynamics of the Party System: Alignment and Realignment of Political Parties in the United States* (Washington, DC: Brookings Institution Press, 1983). For a critique of this literature, see David Mayhew, *Electoral Realignments: A Critique of an American Genre* (New Haven, CT: Yale University Press, 2004). For scholarship showing that national security considerations periodically temper the influence of local constituency interests on legislative behavior, see William G. Howell, Saul P. Jackman, and Jon C. Rogowski, *The Wartime President: Executive Influence and the Nationalizing Politics of Threat* (Chicago, IL: University of Chicago Press, 2013); James Lindsay, "Testing the Parochial Hypothesis: Congress and the Strategic Defense Initiative," *Journal of Politics* 53, no. 3 (1991): 860–876; James Lindsay, "Parochialism, Policy, and Constituency Constraints: Congressional Voting on Strategic Weapons Systems," *American Journal of Political Science* 34, no. 4 (1990): 936–960. Other work suggests that legislators are free to vote according to their own policy preferences when there does not appear to be an acute local economic interest at stake: Sam Peltzman, "Constituent Interest and Congressional Voting," *Journal of Law*

and Economics 27, no 1 (1984): 181–210. Some work on distributive politics further suggests that local constituency interests will be especially salient when legislators make spending decisions that allow for credit claiming but will exercise less influence on spending decisions that do not afford such opportunities: France Lee, "Geographic Politics in the U.S. House of Representatives: Coalition Building and Distribution of Benefits," *American Journal of Political Science* 47, no. 4 (2003): 714–728. Lastly, for scholarship on the transfer of funds among members of Congress, see Eleanor Powell, *Where Money Matters in Congress*, draft book manuscript, University of Wisconsin, 2015.

7. The figures are from Norman J. Ornstein et al., "Table 5-3: House Staff Based in District Offices, 1970–2010" and "Table 5-4: Senate Staff Based in State Offices, 1972–2010," in *Vital Statistics on Congress* (Washington, DC: Brookings Institution and American Enterprise Institute, 2014), http://www .brookings.edu/~/media/Research/Files/Reports/2013/07/vital-statistics -congress-mann-ornstein/Vital-Statistics-Chapter-5--Congressional-Staff-and -Operating-Expenses_UPDATE.pdf?la=en.

8. On myopia among members of Congress, see Gary C. Jacobson, "Running Scared: Elections and Congressional Politics in the 1980s," in *Congress: Structure and Policy,* ed. Mathew D. McCubbins and Terry Sullivan (New York, NY: Cambridge University Press, 1987), 39–81; Morris Fiorina, *Congress: Keystone of the Washington Establishment*, revised ed. (New Haven, NY: Yale University Press, 1989); Anthony King, *Running Scared: Why American Politicians Campaign Too Much and Govern Too Little* (New York, NY: Free Press, 1997).

9. For an extended analysis of Congress's approach to the bureaucracy, see Terry M. Moe, "The Politics of Bureaucratic Structure," in *Can the Government Govern?,* ed. John E. Chubb and Paul E. Peterson (Washington, DC: Brookings Institution Press, 1989), 267–329. See also David Epstein and Sharyn O'Halloran, *Delegating Powers: A Transaction Cost Politics Approach to Policy Making Under Separate Powers* (New York, NY: Cambridge University Press, 1999). For the figures cited in the text on duplication and overlap, see US Government Accountability Office, *Multiple Employment and Training Programs: Providing Information on Colocating Services and Consolidating Administrative Structures Could Promote Efficiencies,* GAO-11-92, January 13, 2011, http://www.gao.gov/assets/320/314551.pdf; Paul C. Light, "Has the Federal Government Become an 'Awful Spectacle'?," United States House of

Representatives Committee on Oversight and Government Reform, February 15, 2012. For an analysis of the politics of food stamps, see John Ferejohn, "Logrolling in an Institutional Context: A Case Study of Food Stamp Legislation," in *Congress and Policy Change,* ed. Gerald C. Wright (Flemington, NJ: Agathon Press, 1986), 223–253.

10. James Snyder and Tim Groseclose, "Estimating Party Influence in Congressional Roll-Call Voting," *American Journal of Political Science* 44, no. 2 (2000): 193–211; Stephen Ansolabehere, James Snyder, and Charles Stewart, "The Effects of Party and Preferences on Congressional Roll-Call Voting," *Legislative Studies Quarterly* 26, no. 4 (2001): 533–572; Thomas Stratmann, "Congressional Voting over Legislative Careers: Shifting Positions and Changing Constraints," *American Political Science Review* 94, no. 3 (2000): 665–676; Joshua Clinton, "Representation in Congress: Constituents and Roll Calls in the 106th House," *Journal of Politics* 68, no. 2 (2006): 397–409.

11. On changes in the American party system during the postwar era, see John H. Aldrich, *Why Parties? A Second Look* (Chicago, IL: University of Chicago Press, 2011); Mark D. Brewer, "The Evolution and Alternation of American Party Coalitions," in *The Oxford Handbook of American Parties and Interest Groups,* ed. L. Sandy Maisel, Jeffrey M. Berry, and George C. Edwards III (New York, NY: Oxford University Press, 2010), 121–142.

12. Gary W. Cox and Mathew D. McCubbins, *Legislative Leviathan: Party Government in the House* (Berkeley, CA: University of California Press, 1993); John H. Aldrich and David W. Rohde, "The Logic of Conditional Party Government: Revisiting the Electoral Connection," in *Congress Reconsidered*, 7th ed., ed. Lawrence C. Dodd and Bruce I. Oppenheimer (Washington, DC: Congressional Quarterly Press, 2001), 269–292.

13. On how leaders and policy entrepreneurs can use parochial inducements to piece together coalitions (but without an emphasis on how these efforts can corrupt the content of policy), see Evans, *Greasing the Wheels.*

14. The White House, Office of the Press Secretary, "Fact Sheet: Immigration Accountability Executive Action" (press release), November 20, 2014, https://www.whitehouse.gov/the-press-office/2014/11/20/fact-sheet-immigration-accountability-executive-action.

15. For background and evidence on the modern politics of immigration, see Darrell M. West, *Brain Gain: Rethinking U.S. Immigration Policy* (Washington, DC: Brookings Institution Press, 2010); Daniel J. Tichenor, *Dividing Lines: The*

Politics of Immigration Control in America (Princeton, NJ: Princeton University Press, 2002); David Jacobson, *Rights Across Borders: Immigration and the Decline of Citizenship* (Baltimore, MD: Johns Hopkins University Press, 1996).

16. West, *Brain Gain*, 41–42.

17. On the special-interest politics of health care during the postwar period, see Paul Starr, *Remedy and Reaction: The Peculiar American Struggle over Health Care Reform*, revised ed. (New Haven, CT: Yale University Press, 2013); Sven Steinmo and Jon Watts, "It's the Institutions, Stupid! Why Comprehensive Health Insurance Always Fails in America," *Journal of Health Politics* 20, no. 2 (1995), 329–372; Jacob Hacker, *The Divided Welfare State: The Battle over Public and Private Social Benefits in the United States* (New York, NY: Cambridge University Press, 2002).

18. Karen Davis, Kristof Stremikis, David Squires, and Cathy Schoen, *Mirror, Mirror on the Wall, 2014 Update: How the U.S. Health Care System Compares Internationally*, The Commonwealth Fund, June 16, 2014; Luca Lorenzoni, Annalisa Belloni, and Franco Sassi, "Health-Care Expenditure and Health Policy in the USA Versus Other High-Spending OECD Countries," *Lancet* 384, no. 9937 (July 5, 2014): 83–92; Christopher Murray and Julio Frenk, "Ranking 37th—Measuring the Performance of the U.S. Health Care System," *New England Journal of Medicine* 362 (January 14, 2010): 98–99.

19. For details on the special-interest politics that surrounded the ACA and profoundly shaped its content, see Starr, *Remedy and Reaction*; Steven Brill, *America's Bitter Pill: Politics, Backroom Deals, and the Fight to Fix Our Broken Healthcare System* (New York, NY: Random House, 2015).

20. US Department of State, "Part 1: Public Acts and Resolutions," *The Statutes at Large of the United States of America, from March, 1913, to March, 1915*, vol. XXXVIII (Washington, DC: US Government Printing Office, 1915), 172–173; Sidney Ratner, *Taxation and Democracy in America* (New York, NY: John Wiley and Sons, 1942), 404; Elliot W. Brownlee, *Federal Taxation in America: A Short History*, 2nd ed. (New York, NY: Cambridge University Press, 2004), 60–61.

21. Eric M. Patashnik, *Reforms at Risk: What Happens After Major Policy Changes Are Enacted?* (Princeton, NJ: Princeton University Press, 2008), 39; Donald L. Bartlett and James B. Steele, "The Great Tax Giveaway: How the Influential Win Billions in Special Tax Breaks," *Philadelphia Inquirer*, April 10, 1988, http://www.barlettandsteele.com/journalism/inq_tax_1.php.

22. Patashnik, *Reforms at Risk,* 53.

23. Jonathan Weisman, "A Republican's Tax Overhaul Envisions Big Changes," *New York Times,* February 26, 2014, http://www.nytimes.com/2014 /02/27/us/politics/sweeping-tax-overhaul-plan-would-bring-big-changes.html; Andrew L. Grossman, "Is the Tax Code Really 70,000 Pages Long?," *Slate,* April 14, 2014, http://www.slate.com/articles/news_and_politics/politics/2014 /04/how_long_is_the_tax_code_it_is_far_shorter_than_70_000_pages.html.

24. US Department of Agriculture, *National School Lunch Program,* September 2013, http://www.fns.usda.gov/sites/default/files/NSLPFactSheet.pdf.

25. For a detailed history of the school lunch program, from which much of this account was drawn, see Susan Levine, *School Lunch Politics: The Surprising History of America's Favorite Welfare Program* (Princeton, NJ: Princeton University Press, 2010).

26. On the more recent special-interest politics of school lunches, see Levine, *School Lunch Politics*; Eliza Krigman, "The Unappetizing Politics of School Lunches: How a Progressive Idea Ended Up Reinforcing Inequality," *The Nation,* June 4, 2008, http://www.thenation.com/article/unappetizing -politics-school-lunches/; Nicholas Confessore, "How School Lunch Became the Latest Political Battleground," *New York Times Magazine,* October 7, 2014, http://www.nytimes.com/2014/10/12/magazine/how-school-lunch-became -the-latest-political-battleground.html.

27. Confessore, "How School Lunch Became the Latest Political Battleground."

28. For a rich and lively source of evidence on this aspect of congressional failure, filled with insightful analysis, see Rauch, *Government's End.*

29. For background on the Jones Act and its politics, see Brian Slattery, Bryan Riley, and Nicolas Loris, *Sink the Jones Act: Restoring America's Competitive Advantage in Maritime-Related Industries,* The Heritage Foundation, May 22, 2014, http://www.heritage.org/research/reports/2014/05/sink -the-jones-act-restoring-americas-competitive-advantage-in-maritime-related -industries.

30. See "Shipping to Puerto Rico," Shipping International, http://puerto-rico .shipping-international.com/rates/san_juan/; "Shipping to the Dominican Republic," Shipping International, http://dominican-republic.shipping-international .com/rates/santo-domingo/; Jaison Abel et al., *Report on the Competitiveness of Puerto Rico's Economy,* Federal Reserve Bank of New York, June 29, 2012,

http://www.newyorkfed.org/regional/puertorico/report.pdf; John Bussey, "Oil and the Ghost of 1920," *Wall Street Journal,* September 13, 2012, http://www.wsj.com/articles/SB10000872396390444433504577649891243975440.

31. Malia Blom Hill, *The Sinking Ship of Cabotage: How the Jones Act Lets Unions and a Few Companies Hold the Economy Hostage,* Capital Research Center, April 7, 2013, http://capitalresearch.org/2013/04/the-sinking-ship-of-cabotage-how-the-jones-act-lets-unions-and-a-few-companies-hold-the-economy-hostage/.

32. Again, see Rauch, *Government's End.* For a broader perspective on how vested interests shield programs and institutions from change, see Terry M. Moe, "Vested Interests and Political Institutions," *Political Science Quarterly* 130, no. 2 (Summer 2015): 277–318.

33. See John Mark Hansen, *Gaining Access: Congress and the Farm Lobbies, 1919–1981* (Chicago, IL: University of Chicago Press, 1991).

34. Patashnik, *Reforms at Risk;* Bruce Gardner, "Plowing Farm Subsidies Under," *National Review,* May 17, 2007, http://www.nationalreview.com/article/220948/plowing-farm-subsidies-under-bruce-gardner.

35. Patashnik, *Reforms at Risk;* Ralph M. Chite, *Farm Bill Budget and Costs: 2002 vs. 2007,* Congressional Research Service, January 29, 2008, http://nationalaglawcenter.org/wp-content/uploads/assets/crs/RS22694.pdf.

36. For more information, see Patashnik, *Reforms at Risk;* Marc F. Bellemare and Nicholas Carnes, "Why Do Members of Congress Support Agricultural Protection?," *Food Policy* 50 (2015): 20–34.

37. On the history of the AFDC, the widespread criticisms of the program, and the politics of attempted reform prior to new legislation in 1996, see, e.g., Steven Teles, *Whose Welfare? AFDC and Elite Politics* (Lawrence, KS: University Press of Kansas, 1996); Lawrence M. Mead, *The New Politics of Poverty: The Nonworking Poor in America* (New York, NY: Basic Books, 1992); Brian Steensland, *The Failed Welfare Revolution: America's Struggle over Guaranteed Income Policy* (Princeton, NJ: Princeton University Press, 2008).

38. See especially Steensland, *The Failed Welfare Revolution.*

39. Mead, *The New Politics of Poverty,* 4. On the politics of TANF's adoption, see R. Kent Weaver, *Ending Welfare as We Know It* (Washington, DC: Brookings Institution Press, 2000).

40. On the politics of American education, including NCLB, see Terry M. Moe, *Special Interest: Teachers Unions and America's Public Schools* (Brook-

ings Institution Press, 2011); Moe, "Vested Interests and Political Institutions." On the politics of NCLB's adoption, see Patrick McGuinn, *No Child Left Behind and the Transformation of Federal Education Policy* (Lawrence, KS: University Press of Kansas, 2006); Jesse H. Rhodes, *An Education in Politics: The Origin and Evolution of No Child Left Behind* (Ithaca, NY: Cornell University Press, 2012).

41. On the problems with NCLB, see, e.g., Caroline Hoxby, "Inadequate Yearly Progress: Unlocking the Secrets of NCLB," *Education Next 5*, no. 3 (Summer 2005): 46–51; Brian Resnick, "The Mess of No Child Left Behind," *The Atlantic*, December 16, 2011, http://www.theatlantic.com/national/archive /2011/12/the-mess-of-no-child-left-behind/250076/.

42. For a broader analysis, see Moe, "Vested Interests and Political Institutions." For the details, see Valerie Strauss, "Why Obama's NCLB Waivers Aren't What He Says They Are," *Washington Post*, February 10, 2012, https://www .washingtonpost.com/blogs/answer-sheet/post/why-obamas-nclb-waivers -arent-what-he-says-they-are/2012/02/09/gIQA3Mbw2Q_blog.html; Valerie Strauss, "What Was Missing—Unfortunately—in the No Child Left Behind Debate," *Washington Post*, July 17, 2015, https://www.washingtonpost.com /news/answer-sheet/wp/2015/07/17/what-was-missing-unfortunately-in-the -no-child-left-behind-debate/; Maggie Severns, "The Plot to Overhaul No Child Left Behind," *Politico*, January 2, 2015, http://www.politico.com/story /2015/01/the-plot-to-overhaul-no-child-left-behind-113857.

43. Emmarie Huetteman, "Senate Approves Overhaul of No Child Left Behind," *New York Times*, December 9, 2015, http://www.nytimes.com /2015/12/10/us/politics/senate-approves-overhaul-of-no-child-left-behind-law .html?_r=0.

44. On how and why the unions and the districts are more powerful at lower levels of government, see Moe, *Special Interest*; also Moe, "Vested Interests and Political Institutions."

45. Moe, "The Politics of Bureaucratic Structure"; Jack H. Knott and Gary J. Miller, *Reforming Bureaucracy: The Politics of Institutional Choice* (Englewood Cliffs, NJ: Prentice-Hall, 1987).

46. For more details on how Congress shapes the bureaucracy, see Moe, "The Politics of Bureaucratic Structure"; Matthew D. McCubbins, Roger G. Noll, and Barry R. Weingast, "Administrative Procedures as Instruments of Political Control," *Journal of Law, Economics, and Organization* 3, no. 2

(Autumn 1987): 243–277; David Epstein and Sharyn O'Halloran, *Delegating Powers* (New York, NY: Cambridge University Press, 1999); John Huber and Charles Shipan, *Deliberate Discretion?* (New York, NY: Cambridge University Press, 2002); William G. Howell and David Lewis, "Agencies by Presidential Design," *Journal of Politics* 64, no. 4 (November 2002): 1095–1114.

47. Moe, "The Politics of Bureaucratic Structure."

48. Paul Light, *The True Size of Government* (Washington, DC: Brookings Institution Press, 1999).

49. For more information, see Suzanne Mettler, *The Submerged State: How Invisible Government Policies Undermine American Democracy* (Chicago, IL: University of Chicago Press, 2011); John J. DiIulio Jr., "Facing Up to Big Government," *National Affairs,* Spring 2012, http://www.nationalaffairs.com/publications/detail/facing-up-to-big-government.

50. Stephen Teles, "Kludgeocracy in America," *National Affairs,* Fall 2013, http://www.nationalaffairs.com/publications/detail/kludgeocracy-in-america.

51. Take, for example, the Supreme Court's recasting of the Affordable Care Act in 2012. The Court held that the federal government had no right to require state governments to add low-income citizens to the Medicaid rolls—and in so deciding, it gutted a key provision of the legislation essential for bringing about universal coverage, and it left millions of low-income people without health insurance when many state governments then refused to enroll them in Medicaid voluntarily. Whatever coherence the ACA initially had as a health-care reform, then, was shredded by the Supreme Court. This kind of thing happens all the time. No one can stop judges from imposing their own preferences on public policy because they are authorized under the Constitution to do what they are doing. Again, welcome to separation of powers.

Chapter 3: The Promise of Presidential Leadership

1. The Interregional Highway Committee's 1941 report, *Interregional Highways,* investigated five possible interstate highway systems. The committee ultimately recommended the third largest, which spanned 33,920 miles in length. The proposed system would have connected all cities with more than three hundred thousand residents and many cities of just over one hundred thousand residents. More than 4,400 of the proposed miles would have been located within city boundaries. The committee also recognized the benefits of

additional circumferential and distributing routes within metropolitan areas, which added upward of five thousand miles of supplemental roads. Congressional Research Service, *Federal Aid to Roads and Highways Since the 18th Century: A Legislative History,* by John Williamson, January 6, 2012, https://www.fas.org/sgp/crs/misc/R42140.pdf; National Interregional Highway Committee, *Interregional Highways,* H.R. Rep. No. 379, at ix (1944).

2. Gary T. Schwartz, "Urban Freeways and the Interstate System," *Southern California Law Review* 49, no. 2 (March 1976): 406–513.

3. In a July 12, 1954, address to a conference of state governors in Bolton Landing in Lake George, New York, the president planned to launch a major highway initiative. Due to the death of his sister-in-law, Eisenhower was unable to attend the event, so Vice President Richard Nixon stepped in to deliver the president's message. The full contents of the speech are available at Richard Nixon, "Address of Vice President Richard Nixon to the Governors Conference Lake George, New York—July 12, 1954," US Department of Transportation, Federal Highway Administration, http://www.fhwa.dot.gov/infrastructure/rw96m.cfm, last updated October 8, 2013.

4. Quoted in Richard F. Weingroff, "Federal-Aid Highway Act of 1956: Creating the Interstate System," *Public Roads* 60, no. 1 (Summer 1996), US Department of Transportation, Federal Highway Administration, http://www.fhwa.dot.gov/publications/publicroads/96summer/p96su10.cfm. Eisenhower's committee went on to recommend that the federal government pick up most of the tab. To finance the system, a newly established Federal Highway Corporation would issue bonds worth $25 billion. Revenue from gas taxes, it was thought, would pay down the bonds over thirty years.

5. Richard F. Weingroff, "Kill the Bill: Why the U.S. House of Representatives Rejected the Interstate System in 1955," US Department of Transportation, Federal Highway Administration, October 15, 2013, http://www.fhwa.dot.gov/infrastructure/killbill.cfm.

6. This report, formally titled *General Location of National System of Interstate Highways,* contained a national map of the entire interstate highway system. For major metropolitan areas, plans were established for an "inner belt" encircling all or part of the downtown areas, an "outer belt" encircling all or part of the entire metropolis, and one or more "radial" freeways leading outward from the inner belt. In a typical medium-size metropolitan area, the proposed interstate system split in two as it approached the city, one branch

going through the city and the other around it, with the two branches then reuniting at a point beyond the city. For smaller cities, a single freeway "spur" was meant to connect the city with the interstate. Schwartz, "Urban Freeways and the Interstate System."

7. On the national perspectives that orient presidents, see William G. Howell, Saul Jackman, and Jon Rogowski. *The Wartime President: Executive Influence and the Nationalizing Politics of Threat* (Chicago, IL: University of Chicago Press); Woodrow Wilson, *Constitutional Government in the United States* (New York, NY: Columbia University Press, 1908); Elena Kagan, "Presidential Administration," *Harvard Law Review* 114 (2001): 2245–2385.

8. Stephen Skowronek, *The Politics Presidents Make: Leadership from John Adams to Bill Clinton* (New York, NY: Belknap Press, 1997), 5.

9. On the expectations surrounding the presidency, see Dennis M. Simon, "Public Expectations of the President," in *The Oxford Handbook of the American Presidency,* ed. George Edwards and William G. Howell (New York, NY: Oxford University Press, 2009), 135–159.

10. On the importance of legacy for understanding presidential behavior, see Terry M. Moe, "Presidents, Institutions, and Theory," in *Researching the Presidency: Vital Questions, New Approaches,* ed. George C. Edwards III, John H. Kessel, and Bert A. Rockman (Pittsburgh, PA: University of Pittsburgh Press, 1993), 337–386. See also Skowronek, *The Politics Presidents Make;* Marc Landy and Sidney Milkis, *Presidential Greatness* (Lawrence, KS: University Press of Kansas, 2000).

11. For arguments bearing on the president's holistic perspective on policy and government, see Terry M. Moe, "The Politicized Presidency," in *The New Direction in American Politics,* ed. John E. Chubb and Paul E. Peterson (Washington, DC: Brookings Institution Press, 1985), 235–271; Terry M. Moe, "The Politics of Bureaucratic Structure," in *Can the Government Govern?,* ed. John E. Chubb and Paul E. Peterson (Washington, DC: Brookings Institution Press, 1989), 267–329; and Moe, "Presidents, Institutions, and Theory."

12. Lyndon B. Johnson, "Speech Before Congress on Voting Rights (March 15, 1965)," The Miller Center, University of Virginia, http://millercenter.org/president/speeches/speech-3386.

13. Michael Beschloss, "In His Final Days, LBJ Agonized Over His Legacy," The Rundown (blog), *PBS NewsHour,* December 4, 2012, http://www.pbs.org/newshour/rundown/lbjs-last-interview/.

14. Stanley I. Kutler, *Abuse of Power: The New Nixon Tapes* (New York, NY: Touchstone, 1997), xiv.

15. Kate Zernike, "Bush's Legacy vs. the 2008 Election," *New York Times*, January 14, 2007, http://www.nytimes.com/2007/01/14/weekinreview/14zernike .html; George W. Bush, *Decision Points* (New York, NY: Random House, 2010), 122.

16. Arthur M. Schlesinger Sr., "Historians Rate U.S. Presidents," *Life*, November 1, 1948, 65–66; Arthur M. Schlesinger Jr., "Rating the Presidents: Washington to Clinton," *Political Science Quarterly* 112, no. 2 (Summer 1997): 179–190. For a recent poll, see, e.g., Brandon Rottinghaus and Justin S. Vaughn, "Measuring Obama Against the Great Presidents," FixGov: Making Government Work (blog), *Brookings*, February 13, 2015, http://www.brookings .edu/blogs/fixgov/posts/2015/02/13-obama-measuring-presidential-greatness -vaughn-rottinghaus. See also "American President: A Reference Resource," The Miller Center, University of Virginia, http://millercenter.org/president; "The Presidents," *American Experience*, PBS, http://www.pbs.org/wgbh/american experience/collections/presidents/.

17. Franklin Roosevelt, "Dedication of the Franklin D. Roosevelt Library," June 30, 1941, Box 2-24, Master Speech File, 1898–1945, Franklin D. Roosevelt Presidential Library & Museum, quoted in Cynthia Koch and Lynn Bassanese, "Roosevelt and His Library," *Prologue* 33, no. 2 (Summer 2001), http:// www.archives.gov/publications/prologue/2001/summer/roosevelt-and-his -library-1.html.

18. Karen Davis, Kristof Stremikis, David Squires, and Cathy Schoen, *Mirror, Mirror on the Wall: How the Performance of the U.S. Health Care System Compares Internationally*, The Commonwealth Fund, June 2014, http://www .commonwealthfund.org/~/media/files/publications/fund-report/2014/jun /1755_Davis_Mirror_Mirror_2014.pdf; Congressional Budget Office, *Insurance Coverage Provisions of the Affordable Care Act—CBO's March 2015 Baseline*, March 2015, https://www.cbo.gov/sites/default/files/cbofiles/attachments/439 00-2015-03-ACAtables.pdf.

19. Much of what follows in this section is based on the following accounts of the history and politics of health policy reform: Paul Starr, *Remedy and Reaction: The Peculiar American Struggle over Health Care Reform* (New Haven, CT: Yale University Press, 2011); Jacob Hacker, *The Road to Nowhere: The Genesis of President Clinton's Plan for Health Security* (Princeton, NJ:

Princeton University Press, 1999); Sven Steinmo and Jon Watts, "It's the Institutions, Stupid! Why Comprehensive National Health Insurance Always Fails in America," *Journal of Health Politics, Policy, and Law* 20, no. 2 (Summer 1995): 329–372; James Morone, *The Democratic Wish: Popular Participation and the Limits of American Government* (New York, NY: Basic Books, 1990).

20. Harry Truman, "Special Message to the Congress Recommending a Comprehensive Health Program," November 19, 1945, Public Papers of the Presidents: Harry S Truman, 1945–1953, Harry S. Truman Library & Museum, http://www.trumanlibrary.org/publicpapers/index.php?pid=483.

21. James Sundquist, *Politics and Policy: The Eisenhower, Kennedy, and Johnson Years* (Washington, DC: Brookings Institution Press, 1968), 314.

22. On the legislative politics of these unusually productive years, including the politics of Medicare, see (in addition to the works cited earlier) Julian E. Zelizer, *The Fierce Urgency of Now: Lyndon Johnson, Congress, and the Battle for the Great Society* (New York, NY: Penguin Press, 2015).

23. Steinmo and Watts, "It's the Institutions, Stupid!," 348.

24. Harold Schmeck, "Nixon Sees Passage in '74 of a Health Insurance Plan; Kennedy Voices Doubts," *New York Times,* February 6, 1974, 16.

25. Steinmo and Watts, "It's the Institutions, Stupid!," 353.

26. Ibid., 359.

27. On the politics surrounding the Clinton health-care plan, see Paul Starr, "What Happened to Health Care Reform?," *The American Prospect,* November 19, 2001, 20–31.

28. The politics and special-interest influence that shaped the ACA are vividly described in Steven Brill, *America's Bitter Pill: Money, Politics, Backroom Deals, and the Fight to Fix Our Broken Healthcare System* (New York, NY: Random House, 2015).

29. US Department of the Interior and US Geological Survey, *Trends in Hydraulic Fracturing Distributions and Treatment Fluids, Additives, Proppants, and Water Volumes Applied to Wells Drilled in the United States from 1947 Through 2010—Data Analysis and Comparison to the Literature,* by Tanya J. Gallegos and Brian A. Varela, Scientific Investigations Report 2014–5131, US Geological Survey (Reston, Virginia, 2015), http://pubs.usgs.gov/sir /2014/5131/pdf/sir2014-5131.pdf; US Energy Information Administration, *Short Term Energy Outlook,* July 2015, http://www.eia.gov/forecasts/steo /archives/Jul15.pdf; Marcelo Prince and Carlos A. Tovar, "How Much U.S. Oil

and Gas Comes from Fracking?," Corporate Intelligence (blog), *Wall Street Journal*, April 1, 2015, http://blogs.wsj.com/corporate-intelligence/2015/04/01 /how-much-u-s-oil-and-gas-comes-from-fracking/; Chad Fraser, "EOG Resources: Pumping Out Gains," *Investing Daily*, March 12, 2014, http://www .investingdaily.com/19724/eog-resources-pumping-out-gains/.

30. See, most recently, US Environmental Protection Agency, *Assessment of the Potential Impacts of Hydraulic Fracturing for Oil and Gas on Drinking Water Resources (External Review Draft)*, EPA/600/R-15/047, June 2015, http://cfpub.epa.gov/ncea/hfstudy/recordisplay.cfm?deid=244651; "Hydraulic Fracturing Background Information," US Environmental Protection Agency, last updated May 9, 2012, http://water.epa.gov/type/groundwater/uic/class2 /hydraulicfracturing/wells_hydrowhat.cfm.

31. Daniel Yergin, *The Prize: The Epic Quest for Oil, Money and Power* (New York, NY: Simon and Schuster, 1991); Brian Resnick, "What America Looked Like: The 1970s Gas Crisis," *The Atlantic*, May 31, 2012, http://www .theatlantic.com/national/archive/2012/05/what-america-looked-like-the-1970s -gas-crisis/257837/.

32. "Petroleum & Other Liquids," US Energy Information Administration, released July 30, 2015, http://www.eia.gov/dnav/pet/hist/LeafHandler.ashx?n =pet&s=mcrimus2&f=m.

33. Richard Nixon, "Address to the Nation About Policies to Deal with the Energy Shortage," November 7, 1973, The American Presidency Project, University of California, Santa Barbara, http://www.presidency.ucsb.edu/ws/?pid =4034; Gerald Ford, "Statement on the Energy Policy and Conservation Act," December 22, 1975, The American Presidency Project, University of California, Santa Barbara, http://www.presidency.ucsb.edu/ws/?pid=5452.

34. "Energy and Environment, 1975 Overview," in *CQ Almanac 1975*, 31st ed. (Washington, DC: Congressional Quarterly, 1976), 173–176, http:// library.cqpress.com/cqalmanac/document.php?id=cqal75-1213502.

35. Jimmy Carter, *Keeping Faith: Memoirs of a President* (New York, NY: Bantam Books, 1982), 92; Jimmy Carter, "Address to the Nation on Energy (April 18, 1977)," The Miller Center, University of Virginia, http://millercenter .org/scripps/archive/speeches/detail/3398.

36. Ian Ostrander and William Lowry, "Oil Crises and Policy Continuity: A History of Failure to Change," *Journal of Policy History* 24, no. 3 (2012): 384–404; Carter, "Address to the Nation on Energy (April 18, 1977)."

37. Victor McFarland, "The Oil Crisis of the 1970s: An International History," (paper presented at the Spring Fellows Conference at the Miller Center of Public Affairs, University of Virginia, May 9, 2013), 34; Carter, *Keeping Faith*, 99.

38. "Energy and Environment, 1978 Overview," in *CQ Almanac 1978*, 34th ed. (Washington, DC: Congressional Quarterly, 1979), 637–638, http://library.cqpress.com/cqalmanac/cqal78-1236634; John Barrow, "An Age of Limits: Jimmy Carter and the Quest for a National Energy Policy," in *The Carter Presidency: Policy Choices in the Post–New Deal Era*, ed. Gary M. Fink and Hugh Davis Graham (Lawrence, KS: University Press of Kansas, 1988), 167; Ostrander and Lowry, "Oil Crises and Policy Continuity."

39. Of course, the word *malaise* never appears in the speech. For elaboration on the surprisingly insightful content of the speech, see Kevin Mattson, *"What the Heck Are You Up To, Mr. President?" Jimmy Carter, America's "Malaise," and the Speech That Should Have Changed the Country* (New York, NY: Penguin Books, 2009); "Jimmy Carter," *American Experience*, directed by Adriana Bosch, PBS, first aired November 11–12, 2002, http://www.pbs.org/wgbh/americanexperience/features/primary-resources/carter-crisis/; Barrow, "An Age of Limits," 169–170.

40. Barrow, "An Age of Limits," 170.

41. Robert Mann, *Legacy to Power: Senator Russell Long of Louisiana* (Lincoln, NE: Paragon House, 1992), 360.

42. McFarland, "The Oil Crisis of the 1970s," 25.

43. Congressional Budget Office, *The Outlook for Social Security,* June 2004, https://www.cbo.gov/sites/default/files/108th-congress-2003-2004/reports/06-14-socialsecurity.pdf.

44. Bush and the CBO disagreed about the date by which funds would be exhausted. He argued that the time would come in 2042, while the CBO predicted 2052. "Text of President Bush's 2005 State of the Union Address," *Washington Post*, February 2, 2005, http://www.washingtonpost.com/wp-srv/politics/transcripts/bushtext_020205.html; Jeanne Sahadi, "Bush's Plan for Social Security," *CNN*, March 4, 2005, http://money.cnn.com/2005/02/02/retirement/stofunion_socsec/.

45. William Welch, "AARP 'Dead Set' Against Bush's Social Security Plan," *USA Today*, January 24, 2005, http://usatoday30.usatoday.com/news/washington/2005-01-24-aarp-ss_x.htm; Dan Balz, "Democrats Accuse Bush of

Not Protecting Pensions," *Washington Post*, June 3, 2005, http://www.washington post.com/wp-dyn/content/article/2005/06/02/AR2005060201847.html; "Shields and Brooks Analyze Social Security, DNC" (transcript), *PBS Newshour*, February 4, 2005, http://www.pbs.org/newshour/bb/politics-jan-june05 -sb_2-04/.

46. Peter H. Wehner, "Memo on Social Security," *Wall Street Journal*, January 5, 2005, http://www.wsj.com/articles/SB110496995612018199.

47. William A. Galston, "Why the 2005 Social Security Initiative Failed, and What It Means for the Future," *Brookings*, September 21, 2007, http:// www.brookings.edu/research/papers/2007/09/21governance-galston.

48. This was true even though young Americans supported Bush's proposal ("Poll: College Students Like Private Account Idea," *Harvard Gazette*, April 21, 2005, http://news.harvard.edu/gazette/2005/04.21/09-iop.html). Polls indicated that older people were against it, however, despite Bush's protestations that it would not affect their benefits (Jonathan Weisman, "Skepticism of Bush's Social Security Program Is Growing," *Washington Post*, March 15, 2005, http://www .washingtonpost.com/wp-dyn/articles/A35231-2005Mar14.html).

49. Jim VandeHei and Mike Allen, "In GOP, Resistance on Social Security," *Washington Post*, January 11, 2005.

50. Karl Rove, *Courage and Consequence: My Life as a Conservative in the Fight* (New York, NY: Threshold Editions, 2010), 409.

51. "Press Conference of the President" (press release), The White House, Office of the Press Secretary, April 28, 2005, http://georgewbush-whitehouse .archives.gov/news/releases/2005/04/20050428-9.html.

52. "Candidate Bush Returns," *The Economist*, March 10, 2005, http:// www.economist.com/node/3749881; Gayle L. Reznik, Dave Shoffner, and David A. Weaver, "Coping with the Demographic Challenge: Fewer Children and Living Longer," *Social Security Bulletin* 66, no. 4 (2005/2006), http://www.ssa .gov/policy/docs/ssb/v66n4/v66n4p37.html.

53. Bush, *Decision Points*; David E. Sanger, "2006 Is So Yesterday," *New York Times*, January 1, 2006, http://www.nytimes.com/2006/01/01/weekinreview/01 sanger.html; Iwan Morgan, introduction to *Assessing George W. Bush's Legacy: The Right Man?*, ed. Iwan Morgan and Philip John Davies (New York, NY: Palgrave Macmillan, 2010), 4.

54. Justin Gillis, "2015 Likely to Be the Hottest Year Ever Recorded," *New York Times*, October 21, 2015, http://www.nytimes.com/2015/10/22/science

/2015-likely-to-be-hottest-year-ever-recorded.html; "Global Warming Fast Facts," *National Geographic News*, updated June 14, 2007, http://news.national geographic.com/news/2004/12/1206_041206_global_warming.html; Intergovernmental Panel on Climate Change, "Summary for Policymakers," in *Climate Change 2007: The Physical Science Basis, Contribution of Working Group 1 to the Fourth Assessment Report of the Intergovernmental Panel on Climate Change,* ed. S. Solomon et al. (Cambridge, UK: Cambridge University Press, 2007), http://www.ipcc.ch/pdf/assessment-report/ar4/wg1/ar4-wg1-spm.pdf; Justin Gillis, "Climate Body Cites Near Certainty on Global Warming," *New York Times,* August 19, 2013, http://www.nytimes.com/2013/08/20/science/earth/extremely -likely-that-human-activity-is-driving-climate-change-panel-finds.html.

55. According to a January 2015 Pew Research Survey, 54 percent of Democrats think climate change is a top priority for the government, compared to 15 percent of Republicans. For trends in the partisan differences on this and other environmental and energy issues, see http://www.pewresearch.org/key -data-points/environment-energy-2/. For additional research on public opinion and climate change, see Stephen Ansolabehere and David Konisky, *Cheap and Clean: How Americans Think About Energy in the Age of Global Warming* (Cambridge, MA: The MIT Press, 2014); Anthony Leiserowitz et al., *Climate Change in the American Mind,* Yale Program on Climate Change Communication, October 2015, http://environment.yale.edu/climate-communication /files/Climate-Change-American-Mind-October-2015.pdf; Bruce Stokes, Richard Wike, and Jill Carle, *Global Concern About Climate Change, Broad Support for Limiting Emissions,* Pew Research Center, November 2015, http://www .pewglobal.org/files/2015/11/Pew-Research-Center-Climate-Change-Report -FINAL-November-5-2015.pdf.

56. Obama for America, *Change We Can Believe In: Barack Obama's Plan to Renew America's Promise* (New York, NY: Random House, 2008), 71.

57. "House Reaches Milestone with Cap-and-Trade Climate Change Bill," in *CQ Almanac 2009,* 65th ed., ed. Jan Austin, 10-3-10-7 (Washington, DC: CQ-Roll Call Group, 2010), http://library.cqpress.com/cqalmanac/cqal09-1183 -59541-2251356; Eric Pooley, *The Climate War: True Believers, Power Brokers, and the Fight to Save the Earth* (New York, NY: Hyperion, 2010), 396.

58. "Press Conference by the President" (press release), The White House, Office of the Press Secretary, June 23, 2009, http://www.whitehouse.gov/the _press_office/Press-Conference-by-the-President-6-23-09/; "Remarks by the

President in State of the Union Address" (press release), The White House, Office of the Press Secretary, January 27, 2010, http://www.whitehouse.gov /the-press-office/remarks-president-state-union-address; Office of Management and Budget, *Budget of the U.S. Government, Fiscal Year 2011* (Washington, DC: US Government Printing Office, 2010), http://www.gpo.gov/fdsys /pkg/BUDGET-2011-BUD/pdf/BUDGET-2011-BUD.pdf.

59. Darren Samuelsohn, "Kerry, Lieberman to End Suspense with Climate Bill Rollout Today," *New York Times,* May 12, 2010, http://www.nytimes.com /cwire/2010/05/12/12climatewire-kerry-lieberman-to-end-the-suspense-with -cli-19936.html.

60. Ryan Lizza, "As the World Burns," *The New Yorker,* October 11, 2010, http://www.newyorker.com/magazine/2010/10/11/as-the-world-burns.

61. "Dead Aim: Joe Manchin for West Virginia TV Ad," October 9, 2010, http://www.youtube.com/watch?v=xIJORBRpOPM; "State Energy Consumption Estimates, 1960 Through 2013," US Energy Information Administration, DOE/EIA-0214(2013), July 2015, https://www.eia.gov/state/seds/sep_use/notes /use_print.pdf.

62. Lizza, "As the World Burns"; "Blanche Lincoln: Top 20 Contributors, 2005–2010," Open Secrets, http://www.opensecrets.org/politicians/contrib.php ?cycle=2010&cid=n00008092&type=I; Clean Energy Partnerships Act of 2009, S.2729, 111th Congress (2009), http://beta.congress.gov/bill/111th-congress/ senate-bill/2729; National Milk Producers Foundation, "Letter to Senators Stabenow, Harkin, Baucus, and Klobuchar," November 4, 2009, http://www .nmpf.org/files/file/Stabenow-Nov09-NMPFlt.pdf.

63. John Broder. "'Cap and Trade' Loses Its Standing as Energy Policy of Choice," *New York Times,* March 25, 2010, http://www.nytimes.com/2010 /03/26/science/earth/26climate.html.

64. Executive Office of the President, *The President's Climate Action Plan,* June 2013, http://www.whitehouse.gov/sites/default/files/image/president27s climateactionplan.pdf.

65. "Remarks by the President in Announcing the Clean Power Plan," The White House, Office of the Press Secretary, August 3, 2015, https://www.white house.gov/the-press-office/2015/08/03/remarks-president-announcing-clean -power-plan. See also Coral Davenport and Gardiner Harris, "Obama to Unveil Tougher Climate Plan with His Legacy in Mind," *New York Times,* August 2, 2015.

66. Quoted in Scott Horsley, "Obama's Climate Plan Faces Huge Political Challenges," *All Things Considered,* NPR, August 3, 2015, http://www.npr .org/2015/08/03/429065065/obamas-climate-plan-faces-huge-political -challenges.

67. Darren Samuelsohn, "Obama Negotiates 'Copenhagen Accord' with Senate Climate Fight in Mind," *New York Times,* December 21, 2009, http://www.nytimes.com/cwire/2009/12/21/21climatewire-obama-negotiates -copenhagen-accord-with-senat-6121.html; Philip Rucker and Juliet Eilperin, "Obama Sets International Climate Forum," *Washington Post,* March 28, 2009, http://voices.washingtonpost.com/44/2009/03/28/obama_sets_international _clima.html; Elizabeth Kolbert, "Congress Moves to Sabotage the Paris Climate Summit," *New Yorker,* December 4, 2015, http://www.newyorker.com/news /daily-comment/congress-moves-to-sabotage-the-paris-climate-summit.

CHAPTER 4: TOWARD A MORE EFFECTIVE GOVERNMENT

1. For books that examine the president's agenda-setting powers, see Brandice Canes-Wrone, *Who Leads Whom?: Presidents, Policy, and the Public* (Chicago, IL: University of Chicago Press, 2006); Matthew Beckman, *Pushing the Agenda: Presidential Leadership in US Lawmaking, 1953–2004* (New York, NY: Cambridge University Press, 2010); Jeffrey Cohen, *Going Local: Presidential Leadership in the Post-Broadcast Age* (New York, NY: Cambridge University Press, 2009); Samuel Kernell, *Going Public: New Strategies of Presidential Leadership,* 4th ed. (Washington, DC: CQ Press, 2006).

2. A large and long-standing research tradition within political science examines the president's capacity to advance a policy agenda within Congress. See, e.g., Jeffrey Cohen, *The President's Legislative Policy Agenda, 1789–2002* (New York, NY: Cambridge University Press, 2012); George Edwards, *At the Margins: Presidential Leadership of Congress* (New Haven, CT: Yale University Press, 1990); Paul Light, *The President's Agenda: Domestic Policy Choice from Kennedy to Clinton,* 3rd ed. (Baltimore, MD: Johns Hopkins University Press, 1999); Jon Bond and Richard Fleisher, *The President in the Legislative Arena* (Chicago, IL: University of Chicago Press, 1992); Mark Peterson, *Legislating Together: The White House and Capitol Hill from Eisenhower to Reagan* (Cambridge, MA: Harvard University Press, 1990). There also is a rather substantial body of work that examines

the specific influence that presidents glean from the veto power. For a summary of the game theoretic work on the subject, see Charles Cameron and Nolan McCarty, "Models of Vetoes and Veto Bargaining," *Annual Review of Political Science* 7 (2005): 409–435. For select empirical studies of the subject, see Charles Cameron, *Veto Bargaining: Presidents and the Politics of Negative Power* (New York, NY: Cambridge University Press, 2000); Nolan McCarty, "Presidential Vetoes in the Early Republic: Changing Constitutional Norms or Electoral Reform," *Journal of Politics* 71, no. 2 (2009): 369–384; John Gilmour, "Institutional and Individual Influences on the President's Veto," *Journal of Politics* 64, no. 1 (2002): 198–218; Robert Spitzer, *Presidential Veto: Touchstone of the American Presidency* (Albany, NY: State University of New York Press, 1988).

3. Terry M. Moe, "The Politicized Presidency," in *The New Direction in American Politics*, ed. John E. Chubb and Paul E. Peterson (Washington, DC: Brookings Institution Press, 1985), 235–271; Peri Arnold, *Making the Managerial Presidency: Comprehensive Reorganization Planning, 1905–1996* (Lawrence, KS: University Press of Kansas, 1998); Charles Walcott and Karen Hult, *Governing the White House: From Hoover Through LBJ* (Lawrence, KS: University Press of Kansas, 1995); John Hart, *The Presidential Branch* (New York, NY: Chatham House Publishers, 1995); John Burke, *The Institutional Presidency: Organizing and Managing the White House from FDR to Clinton*, 2nd ed. (Baltimore, MD: Johns Hopkins University Press, 2000); Thomas Weko, *The Politicizing Presidency: The White House Personnel Office, 1948–1994* (Lawrence, KS: University Press of Kansas, 1995).

4. In our own scholarship, we have written a good deal about the president's powers of unilateral actions. See, e.g., William G. Howell, *Power Without Persuasion: The Politics of Direct Presidential Action* (Princeton, NJ: Princeton University Press, 2003); Terry M. Moe and William G. Howell, "The Presidential Power of Unilateral Action," *Journal of Law, Economics and Organizations* 15, no. 1 (1999): 132–179. Other prominent book-length treatments of the subject include Philip Cooper, *By Order of the President: The Use and Abuse of Executive Direct Action* (Lawrence, KS: University Press of Kansas, 2002); Kenneth Mayer, *With the Stroke of a Pen: Executive Orders and Presidential Power* (Princeton, NJ: Princeton University Press, 2001); Adam Warber, *Executive Orders and the Modern Presidency: Legislating from the Oval Office* (New York, NY: Lynne Rienner, 2008); Darren Wheeler, *Presidential Power in*

Action: Implementing Supreme Court Detainee Decisions (New York, NY: Palgrave MacMillan, 2008).

5. See, in particular, *United States v. Curtiss-Wright Export Company*, 299 U.S. 304 (1936).

6. In the years since the enactment of the 1974 Trade Act, Congress has altered some of the specific rules that govern fast-track authority. In 2002, for example, it mandated that the president provide a ninety-day notice before beginning trade negotiations. The basics, though, have remained much the same: the president introduces an agreement that Congress must evaluate on an up-or-down basis within a fixed period of time, lest it automatically become law.

7. For more on how the act's empowerment of the president increased trade liberalization, see Michael A. Bailey, Judith Goldstein, and Barry R. Weingast, "The Institutional Roots of American Trade Policy: Politics, Coalitions, and International Trade," *World Politics* 49, no. 3 (1997): 309–338; Michael Hiscox, "The Magic Bullet? The RTAA, Institutional Reform, and Trade Liberalization," *International Organization* 53, no. 4 (1999): 669–698.

8. For more on this history, see Todd Tucker and Lori Wallach, *The Rise and Fall of Fast Track Trade Authority* (Washington, DC: Public Citizen, 2009); Ian Fergusson, *Trade Promotion Authority (TPA) and the Role of Congress in Trade Policy,* Congressional Research Service, June 15, 2015, https://fas.org/sgp/crs/misc/RL33743.pdf.

9. Paul Lewis, "Barack Obama Given 'Fast-Track' Authority over Trade Deal Negotiations," *The Guardian,* June 24, 2015, http://www.theguardian.com/us-news/2015/jun/24/barack-obama-fast-track-trade-deal-tpp-senate. In October 2015, the parties to the TPP agreed on terms, which are slated to go before Congress for a vote in early 2016. See Susan Davis, "Congress Renews Fast Track Bill," *USA Today,* June 24, 2015, http://www.usatoday.com/story/news/politics/2015/06/24/congress-renews-fast-track/29226629/.

10. For discussions on the ways in which delegating trade authority to the president can serve as a check against parochial tendencies within Congress, see Susanne Lohmann and Sharyn O'Halloran, "Divided Government and U.S. Trade Policy: Theory and Evidence," *International Organization* 48, no. 4 (1994): 595–632; I. M. Destler, "U.S. Trade Policy-Making in the Eighties," in *Politics and Economics in the Eighties,* ed. Alberto Alesina and Geoffrey

Carliner (Chicago, IL: University of Chicago Press, 1991), 251–281; "Free Trade," IGM Forum (blog), Initiative on Global Markets, University of Chicago Booth School of Business, March 13, 2012, http://www.igmchicago .org/igm-economic-experts-panel/poll-results?SurveyID=SV_0dfr9yjn DcLh17m. During the nineteenth and early twentieth centuries, it bears recognizing, presidents did not push for liberal trade policy nearly so consistently. Indeed, some presidents promoted staunchly protectionist trade regimes. But it also is not at all clear that liberal trade policy during this period was, in fact, in the nation's interest. Indeed, elite opinion on the matter was highly divided. And so we see how presidents can change their positions on specific policies over the broad arc of American history even while remaining committed to national imperatives.

11. It is because members of Congress represent districts and states that Democratic and Republican legislators have intermittently sought to block free trade. The legislative history of the North American Free Trade Agreement, which in the 1990s eliminated most tariffs and restrictions on trade among the United States, Mexico, and Canada, provides a case in point. NAFTA passed only after a monumental political battle, one that pitted the relatively narrow interests of congressional representatives against the president's commitment to larger and longer interests. The arguments for and against NAFTA did not divide neatly across party lines. As Congressman James Traficant put it, "The NAFTA debate shows there's no damn difference between Republicans and Democrats." (Susan B. Garland, Douglas Harbrecht, and Richard S. Dunham, "Sweet Victory," *Businessweek,* November 28, 1993, http://www.bloomberg.com/bw/stories/1993-11-28/sweet -victory.) Opponents were not necessarily members of the opposition party but instead heralded from states that were especially likely to be negatively affected. Majority Whip David E. Bonior of Michigan, a state with a robust union presence, led the Democratic opposition to NAFTA. Democratic senator Ernest F. Hollings saw NAFTA as an "obvious threat" to textile jobs in South Carolina, his home state. Democratic representative Patsy Mink from Hawaii was concerned about Hawaiian sugar plantation workers because there would be no limit on Mexican sugar exports once all of the agreement was phased in. Marcy Kaptur, a representative from a manufacturing-heavy district in northern Ohio, also expressed concern that NAFTA would hurt women in the textile industry. The final vote in the House was

234 in favor and 200 against; in the Senate, the tally was 61 for and 38 against. Republicans supplied the most support, with 60 percent of congressional Democrats voting against Clinton's initiative. Rather than a battle between parties within institutions, this was a battle within parties and between institutions.

12. In keeping with current practice, votes on appointments would occur, under our arrangement, only in the Senate, while votes on policy would occur in both chambers of Congress.

13. See especially James Sundquist, *Constitutional Reform and Effective Government* (Washington, DC: Brookings Institution Press, 1992); William MacDonald, *A New Constitution for America* (New York, NY: B. W. Huebsch, 1921); William Yandell Elliott, *The Need for Constitutional Reform: A Program for National Security* (New York, NY: Whittlesey House, 1935); James MacGregor Burns, *Deadlock of Democracy: Four-Party Politics in America* (New York, NY: Prentice Hall, 1963); Thomas Mann and Norman Ornstein, *It's Even Worse than It Looks: How the American Constitutional System Collided with the New Politics of Extremism* (New York, NY: Basic Books, 2013); Thomas Mann and Norman Ornstein, *The Broken Branch: How Congress Is Failing America and How to Get It Back on Track* (New York, NY: Oxford University Press, 2008); Robert Kaiser, *Act of Congress: How America's Essential Institution Works, and How It Doesn't* (New York, NY: Vintage Press, 2014); Tom Davis, Martin Frost, and Richard Cohen, *Partisan Divide: Congress in Crisis* (New York, NY: FastPencil Premier, 2014); Lawrence Lessig, *Republic Lost: How Money Corrupts Congress—And a Plan to Stop It* (New York, NY: Twelve Books, 2012).

14. The political science literature is filled with works on the power of agenda control. See, e.g., Thomas Romer and Howard Rosenthal, "Political Resource Allocation, Controlled Agendas, and the Status Quo," *Public Choice* 33, no. 4 (1978): 27–43; Kenneth Sheplse and Mark S. Bonchek, *Analyzing Politics* (New York, NY: W. W. Norton, 1997); Gary W. Cox and Mathew D. McCubbins, *Setting the Agenda: Responsible Party Government in the US House of Representatives* (New York, NY: Cambridge University Press, 2005).

15. Nick Gass, "Obama Attacks Boehner on Immigration Reform," *Politico*, February 26, 2015, http://www.politico.com/story/2015/02/barack-obama -john-boehner-immigration-reform-115528.html#ixzz3fumnbiDu.

16. W. Lance Bennett at the University of Washington and John Zaller at UCLA have both written insightfully about the media's dependence on political elites. See, e.g., Bennett's "Toward a Theory of Press-State Relations in the U.S." *Journal of Communication* 40, no. 2 (June 1990): 103–125 and Zaller's (with coauthor Dennis Chiu) "Government's Little Helper: Press Coverage of Foreign Policy Crises, 1945–1991," *Political Communication* 13, no. 4 (1996): 385–406.

17. Suzanne Mettler, *The Submerged State: How Invisible Government Policies Undermine American Democracy* (Chicago, IL: University of Chicago Press, 2011). See also John J. DiIulio Jr., "Facing Up to Big Government," *National Affairs*, Spring 2012, http://www.nationalaffairs.com/publications/detail /facing-up-to-big-government.

18. *Clinton v. City of New York*, 524 U.S. 417 (1998).

19. Jeffrey M. Jones, "Americans' Trust in Executive, Legislative Branches Down," *Gallup*, September 15, 2014, http://www.gallup.com/poll/175790 /americans-trust-executive-legislative-branches-down.aspx; "Trust in Government Nears Record Low, but Most Federal Agencies Are Viewed Favorably—62% Have Positive View of Federal Workers," Pew Research Center, October 18, 2013, http://www.people-press.org/files/legacy-pdf/10-18-13%20 Trust%20in%20Govt%20Update.pdf; "State Governments Viewed Favorably as Federal Rating Hits New Low," Pew Research Center, April 15, 2013, http:// www.people-press.org/files/legacy-pdf/4-15-2013%20Government%20Release .pdf; "Campaign 2016: Modest Interest, High Stakes," Pew Research Center, April 2, 2015, http://www.people-press.org/2015/04/02/campaign-2016-modest -interest-high-stakes/#opinions-of-obama-congress-and-gop-leaders.

20. Herbert Croly, *The Promise of the American Life* (New Brunswick, NJ: Transaction Publishers, [1909] 1993).

21. For an earlier, and similar, assessment of American political culture, see Louis Hartz, *The Liberal Tradition in America* (New York, NY: Harcourt, Brace, and World, 1955), 9.

22. Indeed, Benjamin Wittes and Pietro Nivola have edited a book by exactly this name: *What Would Madison Do? The Father of the Constitution Meets Modern American Politics* (Washington, DC: Brookings Institution Press, 2015).

23. "Transcript: Ted Cruz's Speech at Liberty University," *Washington Post*, March 23, 2015, https://www.washingtonpost.com/politics/transcript-ted-cruzs

-speech-at-liberty-university/2015/03/23/41c4011a-d168-11e4-a62f-ee74591
1a4ff_story.html.

24. Thomas Jefferson to Samuel Kercheval, July 12, 1816, in *The Collected Works of Thomas Jefferson*, ed. Paul Leicester (New York, NY: G. P. Putnam's Sons, 1904), 11–12.

25. H. W. Brands, "Founders Chic: Our Reverence for the Fathers Has Gotten Out of Hand," *Atlantic Monthly*, September 2003, 108.

Index

Betsy Palay

Terry Moe is the William Bennett Munro Professor of Political Science at Stanford University and a senior fellow at the Hoover Institution.

Robert Kozloff: The University of Chicago

William Howell is the Sydney Stein Professor in American Politics at the University of Chicago.